The Way to Human Perfection

IRH Press

Originally published in Japan
as *Okawa Ryuho Shoki Juyoukouenshu Best Selection 2
- Ningen Kansei e no Michi*
by IRH Press Co., Ltd., in January 2021.

IRH PRESS
New York

ISBN 13: 978-1-958655-20-7
Cover Image: Vitalii Matokha/Shutterstock.com
KieferPix/Shutterstock.com

Printed in Canada

First Edition

BEST SELECTION OF RYUHO OKAWA'S EARLY LECTURES

The Way to Human Perfection

EL CANTARE

Ryuho Okawa

IRH PRESS

Footsteps of Ryuho Okawa's early lectures

1989.7.16 — 1989.11.12

We want to create an ideal world based on both private and public happiness. (From Chapter One)

Chapter One

The lecture on July 16, 1989

New Developments in Success Theory

(At Hotel Nagoya Castle)

The audience listening to the lecture

Chapter Two

The lecture on August 6, 1989

The Way to Human Perfection

(At Sapporo Education and Culture Hall)

First, you must accept the fact that you are living your life thanks to a greater power and the existence of many people.
(From Chapter Two)

The large hall where the lecture was give

Chapter Three

The lecture on September 9, 1989

Love, Nurture, and Forgive

(At Munakata Yurix)

People lining up to get into the lecture hall

No matter how great a gift or ability people have, they cannot be truly strong unless they go through adversity, hardship, or difficulty.
(From Chapter Three)

As you make self-reflection a daily habit, you will be able to immediately reflect on your judgment regarding things you thought, spoke, and heard.
(From Chapter Four)

Chapter Four

The lecture on October 8, 1989

Rediscovering the Eightfold Path

(At Marugame Civic Hall)

Marugame Civic Hall

ıe lecture hall was packed with many people

People purchasing new books and cassette tapes

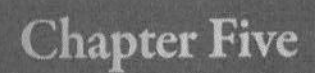

Chapter Five

The lecture on November 12, 1989

What Is Unlimited Love?

(Tokyo Bay NK Hall)

What does it mean to know the true world? It means to know the great love that surrounds us.

(From Chapter Five)

Approx. 6,000 people waiting for the lecture to start

Contents

CHAPTER TWO

The Way to Human Perfection

CHAPTER THREE

Love, Nurture, and Forgive

CHAPTER FOUR

Rediscovering the Eightfold Path

CHAPTER FIVE

What Is Unlimited Love?

Preface

This book takes you back to the lectures I gave almost 32 years ago, in chronological order, as though you attended them in real time. Back then, many non-members also attended my lectures so I spoke using very simple and easy words, making this book an introduction to enlightenment. Those of you who understand Happy Science teachings solely through my books of spiritual messages may find this surprising, but when I read the manuscript of this book, I rediscovered myself who was already a fully-fledged thinker, philosopher, and poet by the young age of 32 or 33.

In this version, many parts that had been deleted by the editorial division are restored. Most of them are about my personal experience, my personal feelings, and my human side. But I thought that it might be OK for those who follow me with the "With Savior" spirit to know that I am also walking the Path with them.

For those of you who are finding the Happy Science teachings too vast to understand, this book explains them in a very easy-to-understand way, so I hope you will read it deeply and thoroughly.

Ryuho Okawa
Master & CEO of Happy Science Group
February 21, 2021

CHAPTER ONE

New Developments in Success Theory

The Fifth Public Lecture of 1989

Originally recorded in Japanese on July 16, 1989
at Hotel Nagoya Castle in Aichi Prefecture, Japan
and later translated into English.

1

The Starting Point of Success Theory

It has been three years since I was last here in Nagoya. I used to live here about three years ago for work, so I feel very nostalgic being here. Yesterday, when I arrived at Nagoya Station, I looked around and noticed that the atmosphere around the station had completely changed. I heard they renovated it for the Design Expo, and indeed, something felt new. The last time I was in Nagoya, I sensed that people here were mainly interested in building a new culture; they seemed to have a desire to establish or create their own culture. I think the Design Expo was held partly for that reason. But here is what I think. Even if people design the shape and appearance of objects, these things will eventually change over the course of time. As for the human mind, however, once it is "designed," it will never get old. It will continue to have an everlasting, eternal life. Once it is formed, it will never disappear.

We are all living eternal lives. I have consistently taught about this theme in the 70 or so books I have published so far (as of the lecture). What I have been saying is as follows: The fact is fact. No evidence can ever overturn this hard fact. But we can offer various resources to support this fact. Each book I publish is based on the single fact that humans have eternal life and are on a path of eternal soul training. I have been publishing books to reveal this basic fact.

Today's lecture is titled, "New Developments in Success Theory." When talking about the theory of success, we must think of us humans as beings that exist in the flow of the great, never-ending river called "eternal life." Without this perspective, we cannot define success. Some of you may say that success means to be recognized in this world, for leading an admirable life for 60 or 70 years. But I do not think this is what success is. Success must be considered from an eternal perspective. Having this perspective is the starting point of living as a human. So no matter how well a theory of success is built, if its starting point is wrong, it will easily crumble, even from a small "earthquake."

Three thousand people are attending this lecture today. Some of you may have read many of my books, while others may not have read any yet. Perhaps some of you are still skeptical. I believe we have a diverse audience. But if you can get a glimpse of the Truth by looking at my expressions and appearance, or hearing the words I speak from this podium, this is what I promise you and declare to all of you:

Humans have eternal life. This is 100 percent true. It is indisputable. Humans were created in this way. If we explore the depths of our minds, we will find that we have lived in different times and places. I have published many books of spiritual messages. The spiritual figures who gave the messages in these books lived as great people in the past. If their lives had ended after they died, it would have been impossible to publish these books of spiritual messages. And yet I am doing so. If you feel I am speaking the truth, it means that eternal life is a fact.

What do I mean by that? All 3,000 of you here will leave this world one day. You will eventually die, but your existence is imperishable. I do not mean "imperishable" in the Christian sense, which is that, "If you do good and believe in the Son of God, you will have eternal life; if not, you will perish like the grass and flowers that are thrown into the fire." All human beings, all lives, have equal value. You are all blessed with eternal life. Yet, how this eternal life expresses itself depends on each person's thoughts and deeds. Your thoughts, motives, and actions will produce results. These results are not only about your life in this world; they also affect you in the afterlife, namely, how you will live in the world you go to after death.

On that premise, today, I will talk about the theory of success under a few frameworks, that is, frameworks for the individual, corporations, and the nation. I will talk about it by roughly dividing the topic into these three levels. But to start off, I would like you to understand the following: The

Success Theory that I teach is different from theories that only teach about superficial, embellished success or success for the purpose of showing off, as you commonly find in books sold at bookstores.

2

Success at the Individual Level —the Fragrance of Enlightenment

First of all, what is success at an individual level? Many people have probably wondered about this. In a way, this success is similar to the happiness we teach at Happy Science. If the concept of success includes the basic idea that humans are living eternal lives, then the meaning of success should perfectly align with the idea of true happiness that we teach. So then, when does success accord with true happiness? There are three basic points I would like you to keep in mind.

For the first point, let me put it in a way that is easy for you to understand. In your several decades of life, if no one tells you, "I'm glad you are here," then you have not been successful. Whether people express it to you in words or not, if they have not thought, "Thank you for being alive," "Thank you for being alive in this era, in this region, in this place, in this time," or "I'm glad you are alive. I'm glad our lives have crossed," then you have definitely not been successful.

To put it in a different way, the worst-case scenario is to be told, "I wish you weren't born." It would mean that there was no point in you being born; your life on earth has not been worthwhile; the fact that you were alive might as well be erased. Please understand this point first. If you say that you have lived a life where people appreciate the fact that you were alive, we must inevitably examine the content of your life.

Then, what is the second point? Unlike the first point which was passive, the second point is more proactive. It is about what you leave behind in this lifetime, whether it be something positive, some kind of work, a visible trace of the efforts you have made, achievements, monuments, or mementos that you can confirm for yourself. It must not be subjective; you must leave behind something that can be recognized objectively.

If you are out in the working world, you can achieve this through your work. Or within a family, if you are a housewife, you can build a utopia in your home—a visible utopia. You can tell whether it is a real utopia or not by looking at the faces of your family members. Look at your children's faces, your husband's, or your parents', and you will come to know. So, the second point is to leave a positive mark on this world in one way or another.

The third point that shows you have succeeded as a person is to have your own philosophy. For many of you, it will be difficult to leave behind a philosophy in the form of a book. Something so difficult is not expected of you. You do not have to write a research paper that others can study.

What I mean by a "philosophy" is the lessons you have learned in life or the lessons you can confidently share with others. "These are the lessons I have grasped throughout my life of 50 or 70 years. I'm sure they will benefit the people who come after me." I want you to learn lessons you can talk about in this way. This may not sound difficult to do, but let me ask you: Do you have your own philosophy? If I asked you to share your philosophy, what would you say? Suppose you were asked, "What lessons have you learned in your life?" Can you explain them in clear, simple words, in a way that would be helpful to others?

A philosophy is not born out of the blue one day. It is something that can only be grasped through studying, contemplating, putting what was learned into practice, and accumulating various experiences. A philosophy will only come from what people have grasped, mastered, and engraved in their minds. Each of you can, or should, possess your own philosophy. Without it, I must say that you have not developed spiritually at all in this lifetime. We have been given a large third dimensional space and are living together with over five billion people in the same era. We are expected to accumulate experiences while on this "Spaceship Earth." If you simply keep your experiences to yourself, you are the only one who will be satisfied. So, rather than keeping them for yourself, you should share them as learning material for other people.

I want you to engrave what you have learned in your mind. The lessons you have engraved in your mind may take the form of teachings, advice, or guidance for others while you are still alive. Even if they do not take form on earth during your lifetime, they can prove beneficial in the world you go to after you pass away—the world I call the Real World.

Many spirits send spiritual messages down to earth through me. But the contents of their messages are not something hard like bricks and concrete blocks. Each and every word of their teachings is a "gem." Their teachings are their philosophies that have clearly gained brilliance through experience and they contain light that they have gained themselves. They are sending you these powerful words of light.

That's right. Just as things come in various sizes, so does enlightenment. Enlightenment has various levels. So, as long as you are living as a human being with a name and a personality, I want you to have your own unique philosophy, even if it may seem inferior to that of someone else. When this philosophy is elevated, it is called "enlightenment."

Indeed, the success that each person achieves should contain "enlightenment." It should come together with their enlightenment. It should have the taste of enlightenment or the fragrance of enlightenment. It is true that enlightenment is not something you can touch or show others. But just as a fruit has its own fruity scent and a flower has its own flowery scent, the enlightenment of each one of you gives off the fragrance of your soul. People can surely smell the difference. When you pass by a peach tree, you will smell peaches. When you pass by a cherry blossom tree, you will smell cherry blossoms. Likewise, the fragrance of each person's enlightenment gives passersby a distinct feeling, aftertaste, and impression.

Just because enlightenment cannot be clearly seen or is not something tangible does not mean you can deny its existence. The fact that each person has a soul means they always emit the fragrance of enlightenment or the rich and mellow scent of enlightenment. And it is the fragrance of each person's enlightenment, as a whole, that determines the atmosphere of this world. If this smell is rotten, if this smell is unpleasant, or if this smell is impure, this world will become a dark, gloomy, and bad-smelling world that no one will want to live in. But when a sweet fragrance fills the air, utopia will manifest. This is not so difficult to imagine.

I spoke about the three points of success at an individual level, incorporating personal enlightenment. This is the basic theory. I want you to understand this basic idea by applying it to your own life. To reiterate, the first step is not to be a burden on other people. Instead of being disliked, be the kind of person whom others will say, "I'm glad you are here." The second step is to make sure you did something of worth in your several decades of life. Leave behind a clear, tangible legacy that enables you to say, "I did this much." Thirdly, engrave life's lessons into your mind and develop them into your own philosophy. When your philosophy is elevated, it becomes your enlightenment; it will bear a fruit called "enlightenment" or bloom into a flower called "enlightenment."

3

Success at the Level of the Corporation —the Virtue of a Leader

Now, let us shift away from the framework of the individual. How can this theory of success be applied to a company or an organization? Please think about this.

Today, there are various companies all across Japan. These companies seem to be prospering and Japan seems to be enjoying unprecedented prosperity. This may be how foreign countries are seeing Japan. However, although capitalist corporations fit well in today's society, they have no heart. This is the biggest flaw. Some people may ask, "Can companies have a heart?" If the word "heart" is unfitting, you could call it "spirit" or a "mindset." In other words, I am talking about a company's purpose.

Each company files articles of incorporation which contain details of its business, and its business objective is to make a profit. It is fine to chase profit, but what is it for? What is in the minds of the people who seek profit? What exactly is the company's objective? What are the people or companies seeking? Have people ever asked themselves these questions? That is what I mean.

I am sure a company teaches its new employees about its business and purpose during orientation. The company has a business objective, and its goal is to make a profit. That is fine. I am not saying that money is evil. Money is a great power if it is used for positive means, and it can make this world a better place. But you must know that profit is essentially neutral in value. Profit itself is neither good nor evil. Whether profit is good or evil is determined by the mindset and motives of the person who uses it and the outcome it brings. Without knowing this, there is no meaning in just increasing the numbers.

Even if a company's balance sheet shows a surplus, when viewed from a spiritual eye, profits spent in good ways are shown in black while profits spent in bad ways are shown in red. What is more, profits that are truly used to make this world better or to create utopia are not written in black but in gold letters. Viewed spiritually, that is how they appear on balance sheets and income statements. If profits are used for other purposes, they are written in red, black, or gray. That is how it is. Without taking this spiritual perspective into account, you will not be able to truly know whether your company's development and prosperity are real. Even if your company prospers, if it disrupts this world and people's lives, and destroys their minds and surroundings, it would be worthless like the dead leaves on a riverside.

What, then, is important? It is the mindset of the company's leader. From now on, no one should be allowed to stay in a leadership position if they are clueless about the mind. I dare say to those of you who have never disciplined your mind: Leave management immediately. Management is not just about ability. Of course, being competent in itself can be a way to give love to others; it allows you to serve the community. However, if you work for your own gain or to be recognized and rewarded, or if your motive is to benefit yourself, then I must say you have no heart.

The word *virtue* is often used to describe the qualities needed to become a manager or leader. But virtue has become an outdated word. People nowadays find it hard to understand this word. Yet, it certainly exists. Let me explain it to you in simple words. A virtuous person is someone who spends the majority of the time in their life thinking about other people's happiness.

Now, all of you, look within your minds. What have you thought about in your few decades of life? Has it mainly been about yourself? You can narrow it down to a typical day in your life. Out of the 24 hours, let's say you are awake for 16 hours. What did you think about in those hours? Was it mostly about yourself? Were you only worried about your personal concerns? You may have sometimes thought of others, but were you thinking about their bad points? Were you full of complaints, criticism, or reproaches? Were you always blaming others or your environment? Such people lack virtue. A virtuous person continuously has loving thoughts toward other people.

In this world, we cannot tell what is inside a person's mind. Unfortunately, the human mind is not transparent in this world whereas in the other world, it is see-through as if looking through glass. We cannot see this now, but any loving thoughts that you have continuously had in your mind will manifest as the light of your soul. This is virtue.

Virtue is not something that can be taken out and shown to everyone. But ask yourself the following questions: How much time did you spend thinking about love for other people without considering your own benefit or the desire for fame or self-preservation? Did you spend your time wishing to make other people happy? The total amount of time you spend doing those things will manifest as virtue.

In my book, *Rojin, Buddha's Mystical Power*, I explained that the light of enlightenment leaks out from within. Likewise, although the mind is not see-through like glass and is covered by the physical body in this third dimensional world, light surely seeps out from it. Light leaks from the mind, as if from inside a silkworm cocoon. This is virtue. How much did you think about others? How much did you think about nurturing, forgiving, and cherishing others? This shows your virtue.

This is my answer for those of you who have no idea what virtue is. Virtue can be explained in many ways, but I have explained it in the simplest way. Fill your mind with love for others. Know that love and virtue are very much akin to each other. Virtue grows into a large gem similar to the way oysters make pearls. The process of a pearl becoming larger is very much like the developmental stages of love that I taught about in *The Laws of the Sun*.

To become a virtuous person, you must be willing to give love to others. Instead of having a give-and-take attitude, it is important to only have a love-that-gives attitude. I have named this kind of love "fundamental love." I have also been teaching that talented people who develop more skills will be able to practice "nurturing love" as they practice giving love. "Nurturing love" is a leader's love; it is a love that teaches and guides others. This stage of love is above the stage of simply giving love. I have said that many leaders of this world practice this type of love. And I have also said that love that is more difficult than "nurturing love" is the stage of "forgiving love."

"Nurturing love" is love practiced by outstanding people. These people can see both the strengths and flaws of others. But at the same time, they develop an acute sense of what is inferior and superior, so they start picking on other people's flaws. Most executives struggle with this issue. When people are at the stage of nurturing love, they can see people's flaws too clearly. They pick up on their subordinates' mistakes and weak points too much. Then, like Machiavelli who wrote *The Prince*, they start to treat people like objects or machines to protect their organization called the "company." They can develop a cold heart in this way.

To overcome this tendency, you need "forgiving love" toward other people. "Forgiving love" is a kind love. It is a feeling of kindness. It is a love that embraces others by forgiving their sins, mistakes, and faults, based on the view that they, too, were created by God and were given life, much like you were. This love arises when your mind has elevated to a religious state.

Then, I stated that above this is "love incarnate," the love of an even greater leader or a great figure. It is the love of someone whose very existence becomes the ethos of the age. Their very presence in that time period is a gospel to humanity. Such a figure exists in any time and in any region. They emit light in all directions. Their love is not one-on-one or aimed at someone in particular. They are simply shining. Like Edison's light bulb, they keep on shining. I call such love, "love incarnate."

The developmental stages of love are the same as the stages of growing in virtue. If I were to point out a difference, I would say that love manifests in actions. Love manifests in people's activities. Love is born between people. Love appears in relationships between people. Thoughts take form and manifest in a visible way through deeds or activities, and we call this action "love." On the other hand, virtue has an emphasis on existence itself, rather than action or activity.

Virtue can also be explained as the profound wisdom that is stored in your mind. When love sublimates and crystallizes into a gem, it becomes virtue. Virtue is rarely used fully. To use an analogy, virtue is like a crystal ball; you can look through it and see its beauty, but you can never touch the inside of it. You can touch the surface of it but not the inside. So virtue is like a crystal ball. Anyone can see it if they try, but they cannot touch it with their hands. This is virtue. Virtue is the holy "existence" within you.

4

Success at the Level of the Nation

Virtuous politics and the parliamentary system

So far, I have talked about the kind of leaders we need at the company level and how they should have virtue. Naturally, this type of discussion should also apply at the national level. Currently, it is election season in Japan. Japanese politics is at a major turning point, and the politicians are unable to tell which direction Japan should head in the future. But if they do not know which way to head, they should neither ask their own little brains nor look to other countries for a model to follow. They must seek God's Will or God's Thoughts.

How does Japan look in God's eyes? Where should Japanese politics head? People need to discuss these issues more seriously. Political parties must not merely compete over the number of votes or seats in the Diet. They must think more seriously. People talk about political issues and corruption, but in the end, these problems boil down to a single point—politics lacks virtue. Politicians lack virtue.

Politicians without virtue cannot see what God is aiming to achieve. It means they do not know which way is the right direction. It means they do not know which direction is the way to true righteousness. This is what it all boils down to. Without knowing which way is the right direction, politicians are striving in their own way. In the eyes of the many citizens who are not working in the field of politics, these politicians appear to be living egoistically for their own benefit with a competitive, selfish mind. If politicians had virtue and could see the direction God stands in, their efforts would be rightfully rewarded and appreciated. But because they lack depth, people think they are working to protect or benefit themselves, or to further their own power. Even if that is not their true aim, the fact that people see them that way means they have lost sight of the essence of politics or the "North Star."

Now, Japan is about to face a great turning point. The next 10 years until the year 2000 will be a great turning point for Japan's future. Many things will happen in the next decade. There may be chaos. However, beyond the chaos, we must return politics to the hands of those who deserve it; in other words, the order and mission of the Real World must be reflected in politics. We must achieve this goal. There is no other goal.

There are several ways to achieve this. Take, for example, the current parliamentary system. I do not think that the two political institutions—the House of Representatives and the House of Councillors—are functioning properly. I do not think that the House of Councillors is necessary. Why do I think so? It is because, essentially, the House of Councillors is supposed to act as the conscience of the legislature so that good, insightful people can apply the "brakes" if the government goes astray. But unfortunately, it is not functioning in this way. The councillors do not seem to be capable of exercising sound judgment. They are just creating delays and inefficiencies in national politics by duplicating the legislative process.

Moreover, electoral democracy is believed to be what democracy is all about, but this is also a big mistake. Electoral democracy is not necessarily highly evaluated from a grander viewpoint. It can prevent the worst from happening and raise politics to a certain level, but the ideal form of politics has never been realized through electoral democracy. That is because the process of finding virtuous people is inconsistent with competition for self-interest and power. It is not compatible with the principle of competition. Virtuous leaders are naturally chosen. They emerge naturally. That is how virtuous people are found. So, we must not treat virtuous people roughly like glass shards that are boiled and stirred in a pot to be recycled. The political system should allow for virtuous leaders to be chosen naturally.

Truly virtuous people cannot emerge and become politicians under today's electoral system. You probably understand the major reasons for this. One reason is that running for office costs money. Another is that being a politician is a very unstable profession. Furthermore, virtuous politicians would not be able to stand working with other politicians who lack awareness. There are many other reasons. So we must be courageous and reform the system in the coming age.

There are several ways to reform it. Here is what I would recommend at this point in time: Divide the House of Representatives into three groups. If the Diet consists of 600 members, for example, then one-third, or 200 of them, should be trained as political experts.

Politicians cannot truly lead the nation if they must work to win an election every two, three, or four years. In recent years, we have been constantly flooded with information so we need experts in every profession. I doubt that short-lived politicians have the ability to lead bureaucrats or lead the opinions of foreign countries in a good direction. If we want to make great achievements as a country, we need experts in politics. So at least one-third, or 200 people, should be trained as experts in politics. They should take a test, but it does not have to be a certification test like the one university students take before graduating. We should allow people with over five years of experience in the working world to take a national test for politicians and be certified. It would test one's expertise in politics, economics, and law. However, on its own, that would be the same as the current system for selecting bureaucrats. So, in addition, I strongly recommend they be tested on their knowledge of the Truth or the teachings of the mind. We want to elect people who have studied this. We want to elect those who have studied both specialized knowledge and the Truth, and to nurture them as political experts. In case some of them become corrupt, a national review could be held every 10 years, like it is for Japanese Supreme Court justices. If they are not disqualified, they can serve until they retire at age 60. This is crucial for leading the country.

For the next third, or the second group of 200 people, I propose "vocation-based democracy," or "democracy by industry," to replace the current House of Councillors. Currently, each industry has its own group. For example, the banking industry has the Bankers Association whose chair is the head of a city bank. There are many industries such as banking, manufacturing, steel, machinery, and oil. So here is my idea: Every four years, each industry elects one person to serve as a Diet member. This person should have experience serving as one of the top people in their industry. These Diet members would be elected by people in their own industries and those who have served their full term of four years would not be reelected. In this way, each industry in turn could send a leader to be a Diet member. This system should replace the House of Councillors. These Diet members could belong to any political party during their terms. They would not be required to work to protect and promote the interest of any particular group. Once they are selected by the people in their industry, they can freely choose which party they will belong to.

The last third, or final group of 200 Diet members, should be chosen by election. Every four years, each of the 47 prefectures should elect two members, which would amount to about 100 members. And the remaining 100 members should be elected nationally.

Thus, there would be three groups: professional politicians, industry-based politicians, and elected politicians. Each group could select one candidate for the position of prime minister. A national referendum would then determine who out of those three will become the prime minister. This approach would allow us to select the best person from various groups. This is the electoral system I recommend at this time. We can prevent politics from becoming unstable by having professional politicians. We can ensure that we have highly competent people in politics by choosing successful businesspeople. And we can bring in new people by filling political seats through elections. I think this is a desirable approach.

The tax system and government services

There is another point I must make now. Currently, the tax system is an issue. Japan's tax system has reached a point where it is clearly wrong in the eyes of God. It is wrong. It is not the desirable approach to taxation. God thinks that the acceptable tax rate in a country is 10 percent; 10 percent from individuals and 10 percent from companies, no more than that. This is the basic rule that has been adapted over a long period of time. Nowadays, a tax rate of over 50 percent is imposed on some individuals, and high taxes are also imposed on companies. As a result, high-income earners have lost the will to work. Businesses have created extra work to save on taxes, which is a waste of time and leaves them less time to work on business development. So, the government should not impose more than 10 percent. They must think and spend within this amount of tax revenue. If this is the limit, they will figure out what they should do, which should be obvious. It is to spend within the level of tax revenue.

What should the government do if they need more money? The Ministry of Finance would distribute money to each ministry out of the revenue collected from the 10 percent tax, but if ministries want to spend more, they should provide their own services and be paid for them. Ministries and agencies must incorporate ways of running a business.

They should earn money for their services if they want to spend more. Then, unnecessary services will naturally be weeded out. If the citizens find no economic value in particular government services, there will be no demand for them. Many services are useless now. Think about it and you will see. They are doing a lot of useless work. These unnecessary services will be completely eliminated while useful services will generate money. Each ministry should earn money by providing good services and making their citizens happy. In this way, ministries can budget and operate within their own income.

Another fundamental mistake is the idea that a budget must be used up within a year or the following year at the latest. Could an idea like this apply to your household or business? Do you spend all of your budget? Will your family be able to survive by doing that? What if you suddenly need to pay a tuition fee or medical bills? What if the economy slides into recession? Naturally, companies save money if they make enough profit, but the government does not. They spend it all because unless they do, they cannot plan their budget for the following year. That is why you see a lot of road work near the end of the fiscal year. It is ridiculous. You may be laughing, but acting this way is unacceptable.

Each ministry can have its own budget, but it should save money and spend it on critical projects every five to ten years. If they have money left, they can invest it. You probably agree.

What is more, there are many unnecessary government agencies. Please excuse me if you are working there. For example, the Ministry of Agriculture, Forestry and Fisheries is not necessary. It should be privatized. They give out several trillion yen in agricultural subsidies, which are almost equal to the income tax collected from salaried workers. They need to adopt company logic. Next is the Ministry of Transport. I cannot see the purpose of it. The government does not operate railways anymore. Government approvals and licenses are no longer necessary. Next, we should consider the Ministry of Posts and Telecommunications. Why do we need them? Private delivery services such as Yamato Transport have developed, so we do not need national postal services. Having a banking agency in the post office that collects money (postal savings) is strange, too, because the Ministry of Finance is also collecting money (taxes). It should be integrated into the Ministry of Finance to be a state-run bank. If they are short on tax revenue, they can make a profit by investing the money they have collected. They should make an effort to fund the budget themselves, but they are failing at this now. Another one is the Ministry of Education. It is fine to have a center that makes guidelines for education, but the rest is unnecessary. The Ministry of

Health and Welfare, too, I am not sure why it exists. The medical insurance premiums are virtually a tax. Because they cannot increase the tax revenue anymore, they take money that way. The Ministries of Foreign Affairs, International Trade & Industry, Home Affairs, and part of the Ministry of Finance may remain, but other ministries should be downgraded to bureaus or small agencies. Then, taxes can be reduced to a great extent.

The Ministry of Finance has given administrative guidance to banks, but banks have made great progress since World War II, protected by the Ministry of Finance. As a result, city banks are making hundreds of billions of yen in ordinary income. Is this acceptable? Should they be allowed to make such profits under governmental protection? It is wrong if you look at the way companies work. If a bank is making large profits, their "product prices" should go down, meaning that interest rates on loans should be lowered. But this does not occur because interest rates have not been deregulated. The ministry protects the banks by setting the same interest rate for all. This is wrong. If banks receive guidance from the Ministry of Finance, they should pay a fee out of their profits, like taxes. If not, they should compete freely in a financially deregulated environment. Some banks may become financially weak by doing so, but that applies to private companies, too. They must streamline their management and offer people lower-priced services. This kind of government protection is wrong. We have passed the postwar period of development, so it is unnecessary now.

Even though there is a lot of needless work, the government continues to have these agencies and impose high taxes. The taxes are only increasing, just like the salaries of civil servants increase every year. This kind of society is wrong. Taxes must be kept at 10 percent, at most. If the government needs more, they should earn money by providing services, and spend within their revenue. Living within your budget is crucial for individuals, too. You must save part of your income. This will build financial power and yield prosperity, like accumulated virtue. This is true at a national level as well.

5
Creating an Ideal World

What I want to say is that, at times, it is important to question things that have been considered the norm. We are aiming to build utopia in the name of the Truth, but this is not limited to the world of the mind. If there is something wrong with the social system, we must point it out.

Please listen carefully and think about this. What does it mean for where you live, your country, or the world, to become better? It means you should become happier and happier, year after year. Otherwise, we cannot say we are on a path to becoming a first-rate country. The value of Truth should work on economic and political levels, as well. It must work to increase people's happiness.

If so, why do you not speak up? Why do you remain seated? We must carry out various activities under the single idea of "happiness." We should not just complain. We should not just criticize for the sake of criticizing. The world must become the way it should be; we need utopia.

Therefore, from this day on, please have two goals. I want you to have two clear goals. What is the first goal? It is called the pursuit of private happiness. Do not mistake this for egotism. The pursuit of private happiness is the pursuit of enlightenment or the pursuit of happiness that comes with enlightenment. It is to experience how your enlightenment affects your surroundings. Enhancing your sense of happiness based on a higher level of enlightenment—this is the pursuit of private happiness, which is a basic theory of Happy Science.

The other is the pursuit of public happiness, which I have not talked about much until now. Do not think about yourself only. Do not think about your spiritual happiness only. Open your eyes more and think about the happiness of others. Think about the happiness of many others in your community and nation. Do not wait for others to do it. Keep a sharp eye out, and be determined to learn and experience many things with passion. Voice your opinions and take action to make the world better. This is a basic starting point, too.

Utopia will not be born unless you, yourself, take action. Do not blame other people, the times, or your country for the lack of utopia. If Japan is not a good place to live, if it worsens year after year, it means each person is not making sufficient effort. We will not settle for personal happiness only. We want to create an ideal world based on both private and public happiness. Creating an ideal world is the final goal of Happy Science. We will work hard, so we hope that you will join our movement.

CHAPTER TWO

The Way to Human Perfection

The Sixth Public Lecture of 1989

Originally recorded in Japanese on August 6, 1989
at Sapporo Education and Culture Hall in Hokkaido, Japan
and later translated into English.

1
The Eternal Ideal

For many of you here in Hokkaido, today's lecture is probably the first one you attend. I am very happy about that. I am glad I was able to come to this northern land at such an early stage of our activities. Actually, this is the first time I have come to Hokkaido. I am giving a lecture on my very first visit here, so today's work will be very memorable for me.

This northern land was one of the places I yearned to visit in my youth because it was on this very land that Kanzo Uchimura, a Japanese Christian leader (1861-1930), and other prominent figures studied in the past. This is something that has been on my mind for over a decade. Even though people may share the same mission, it is difficult for them to meet face-to-face in the same age and location. Decades, centuries, or millennia ago, people with similar aspirations to ours lived, contemplated deeply, and carried out various activities. Just thinking about this fact gives us a lot of courage and hope. In the same way, if my lecture today brings hope to future generations, I would be very happy.

For today's lecture, I have chosen the title, "The Way to Human Perfection." This is a grand topic. It is too vast a topic to cover in just one lecture, so for today, I hope to at least invite you to walk the way to human perfection.

So far, I have already published nearly 80 books (as of the lecture). Many of you may have read them from various angles, but you may still find it difficult to grasp the bigger picture of Happy Science's activities and teachings. If I dare to explain it in simple words, I am giving teachings to create outstanding people in this modern society and, by doing so, change the world for the better. This seemingly simple task was carried out nearly 2,600 years ago in India when Buddha gave teachings to produce enlightened or awakened people. Similarly in China, Confucius taught the way to be a sage 2,500 years ago. Although I would not use the word "sage" in this modern age, what I teach has exactly the same content as his. In other words, the way to be a "sage" is the way to human perfection. As long as you are undergoing soul training as a human being, you must keep walking the way to human perfection. The way to human perfection is an eternal hope and an eternal ideal. That is what I believe.

When viewed from this starting point, if studying at Happy Science does not make you a wonderful person, does not help you improve as a person, or does not change you into an ideal person in the eyes of others, then there is absolutely no reason for Happy Science to exist. When you study at Happy Science, the first thing that should happen to you is positive changes. The kind of miracle we are seeking is not something special but something quite ordinary. We want people to learn the teachings steadily and practice them. And when they take one, two, or three steps forward in their lives, this, in itself, is a miracle. We have this kind of sound attitude as the basis of our thinking and I want you to know it. Of course, if I just focus on making miracles happen, then great miracles will surely occur. It is possible. But I do not like to do such things because I am always thinking about teaching the Truth to many people, including those who will come in 2,000 or 3,000 years' time.

"The age of miracles" is surely wonderful, but after it passes, it will become a myth. Even if many people believe that such an age existed and that extraordinary things happened in the past, they will gradually come to think of them as mere made-up stories or fiction. People will tend to believe that such miracles have nothing to do with their lives. However, I was not born just to deliver messages to people living in the current age. I want to give the same chance of walking the way to human perfection to those who come in 500, 1,000, or 2,000 years' time. That is my hope. This is the reason why I have adopted a very steady, ordinary approach, despite being capable of providing far more mystical content and performing mystical actions.

So I place great emphasis on studying the Truth in this present age while I can speak directly to you. In religion, a movement that focuses on studying the teachings usually arises after the founder has passed away. But in my case, I have started this movement while I can still talk to you directly. This is because I do not want the Way to the Truth to be distorted and also because I want my ideas to take root firmly from an early stage.

It is up to each individual to seek the Way, regardless of which age they are born into. However, the reason why many people are eager to seek the Way is because they are always born together for the same mission. There are no exceptions to this. People are not just born to seek the Way by themselves or to seek the Way individually in different ages. A group of people are born in each age to create the ethos of their age.

To everyone who has gathered here today, I especially want you to know how difficult it is to be born in Japan now, in this age. You have had many chances to be born in Japan in the last few hundred years. You will have a chance to be born here in the future as well. But you chose this present age. You chose this age and this land. That is because many people are being born today to create a new ethos of the age. Because you knew about this before you were born, you could not miss the opportunity to be born in this age, on this land.

Delve deeply into your soul and ask, "Was I born here, in this age by chance?" It cannot be so. You were definitely born because you had a very strong desire to be born now. It is very difficult to be born in this present age. Some people may imagine that it is easy to be born in a certain place at a certain time, but in human history, it is actually extremely difficult to be born at a time when we are about to reach an extraordinary height of civilization. You must never forget that you were born with great expectations from heaven and a great hope for future generations. Without this awareness of the times and a sense of mission, your spiritual discipline in this lifetime will be meaningless. If you fail to see this, all of your studies will be in vain.

Remember that your life today in this age is a manifestation of your passion. The very fact that you are alive at this moment is the result of the passion you have held in your soul for thousands of years.

2

You Are Alive Thanks to a Greater Power

The people who have come to my first lecture in Hokkaido today must have a very strong spiritual connection to the Truth. I am sure you have a very strong yearning in your soul to have been able to come to my first lecture against all odds. This strong yearning does not come from your mind, which you believe to be you. You may believe you have come here out of your own free will, but in truth, certain beings have guided you here. You may not be able to see them or feel them with your physical senses, but they do exist. The world we live in is not just made up of what we can see with our eyes, hear with our ears, or touch with our hands.

From the perspective of the Real World, this third dimensional Phenomenal World we live in is like a fishbowl. This world is like a fishbowl on a desk, and all of you are the "goldfish" swimming around inside it. The freedom of the goldfish is restricted and they have no choice but to swim in the limited world of the fishbowl. When a goldfish jumps out of the fishbowl, it will die. Please know that this illustrates how you are in this world.

You may believe that you are swimming freely and independently in this world. But in truth, there is a being that always encourages you when you have the aspiration and determination to take action for something more valuable, for a higher purpose, or for a greater ideal. That is your guardian spirit, which you may have heard about. Your guardian spirit is not a stranger to you. It is actually a part of your own soul. It may sound odd to hear that your guardian spirit is a part of your soul. It may sound unfamiliar, or even hard to believe. But I will reveal to you the truth about our existence: The entity that is born into this third dimensional world and dwells in this physical body is not the entirety of what we are. Our soul is a much greater entity. It is a greater energy form with greater intelligence.

You may have heard about the subconscious mind. We have a conscious mind and a subconscious mind. It is said that we usually think, judge, and act based on our conscious mind. This is true. But while you perceive life with your conscious mind, there will be times when you come up with an unexpected idea. It could be about your future career or a new project at work. When you are at a crossroads in your life—wondering whether you should advance or retreat, or go left or go right—an idea may come to you.

Some words or ideas may come to you most unexpectedly and out of context. They may spring forth from deep within your mind, or come down to you as if it came from heaven. If not from within you, they may come from someone else, possibly someone close to you. The person may say the words you needed to hear the most. This shows that you are not actually living on your own, although it may seem that way. There are beings that are helping you live and are always with you. This is the reality.

You have probably heard about the infinite power of the subconscious mind. Indeed, your soul has soul siblings in the world beyond this one. Among these soul siblings, the one most suited to guide you and advise you in fulfilling your mission in this lifetime takes on the role of your guardian spirit. This soul sibling could be the one who will be born after you, or it may be your immediate past life. Either way, the one who is most fitting to guide you in your present life is protecting you and guiding you.

To those of you who have come to my lecture for the first time today, I want to ask, what made you come? Perhaps you read my books. But then again, there are many people who have read my books and still did not come. You may have received a flyer, seen a poster, or been invited by a friend. But what actually prompted you to come here? There was, in fact, a being who brought you here. When you understand this truth, you will realize how great a responsibility you have for your own life.

I started receiving spiritual powers eight years ago. But when I look back, I realize that I had already received much guidance prior to that. I could only recognize them after they happened. On various occasions, particularly when I was facing the danger of a downfall, I was guided in many ways. Sometimes, a person's words helped me when I was about to give in to despair. At other times, a sentence in a book caught my eye when I was at a loss. I also failed to achieve self-realization many times, but it turned out that such harsh experiences saved me from going down the wrong path. I only realized afterward that I was being guided in many ways, though I am deeply aware of it now. Perhaps those who lack such awareness only have a shallow view of life.

Although people often talk about human perfection, many are living superficial lives. If I were to ask each person about it, 80 to 90 percent of them would probably say that they are conscious of how other people think of them. They are probably picturing the ideal image of themselves in the eyes of other people. Don't you agree? I think that is how most people are. But I would like to point out that, as long as you need to confirm your own success in the eyes of others, you have not yet reached a lofty state of mind.

Many people will find themselves in this state even at the end of their lives. The higher their position or greater their fame in this world, the more likely they are to assess themselves in light of the views and opinions of others. This seems to be the case now in the world of politics, business, and academia. However, please know that those who try to assess themselves based on external values or criteria are nowhere near human perfection. That is because those people do not know the deep truth about life.

As I just said, we humans are constantly being given many things, even from the world we cannot normally see or perceive. We are guided by many beings every day. We are given many opportunities and many encounters, and presented with different destinies. Those who do not realize this see this world as "a work of clay"; they believe they can "make" their houses and "create" dogs, horses, or humans of their own free will as if playing with clay. But if they believe they can just live as they like and leave this world feeling satisfied, they are mistaken.

In a sense, there is nothing we can truly accomplish on our own. You may be surprised to hear this because, until now, I have mainly taught about the importance of self-discipline based on Self-Power. But the fact is, humans on earth cannot succeed or achieve anything in the truest sense with their power alone. Never forget this.

Why so? To answer this question, you do not even need to think about the spiritual world or the Real World. Just think of your relationships with other people living on earth. You will see that other people are always involved whenever you try to achieve something. They may help you proactively or passively. Some of them may oppose you. Whatever the case, your thoughts and actions definitely manifest as you influence others and vice versa. They cannot be achieved without the presence of others, their reactions, their thoughts, or their actions.

From this perspective, look back on your own journey through life. If you simply think about how well you have done yourself, you have probably forgotten many things. You may be overlooking many favors that have been given to you. You may have worked hard, but many people must have supported you and enabled you to exert yourself. You must not forget about the people who gave you these opportunities.

No matter how competent you may be, you would not be able to accomplish anything if everyone around you tried to stand in the way of your self-realization. For example, I am giving a lecture now, but this would not have been possible if people had tried to prevent me from giving one. I could not have done it with my will alone. I can only do this because there are people who listen to my lectures. What is more, there were also people who helped prepare the venue.

Even if you think you have total freedom to do something, there will always be a condition. This condition—the condition of freedom—arises from the presence of others. Never forget this. When you look at people who are enjoying their freedom fully and are living as they wish, you may admire them as ideal models of human perfection. But that is not right. Those who have truly walked the way to perfecting themselves understand that there is a condition to freedom, which is responsibility. They have truthfully and deeply understood this "conditional freedom." That is why those who have truly achieved more have a deeper sense of gratitude. The higher their positions and the greater the influence they have over others, the more they will come to feel, "This is not my power. This is not done with my power alone."

I want to emphasize this point very strongly as a starting point. First, you must accept the fact that you are living your life thanks to a greater power and the existence of many people. Without accepting this, no matter how you express your thoughts or take action, it will not lead you to true growth as a human.

3
The Great Tree of Life

From a micro perspective, we human beings may appear to be living independently, but the reality is that, when viewed from a macro perspective, humans are part of one gigantic tree of life. An infinite number of roots grow out from this gigantic tree of life; small roots extend from the main root, and even finer capillary-like roots extend from those small roots. The truth is that human souls branch off in this way.

You are one of the smallest hair-like roots of this tree. What would happen if one of those roots hoarded all of the nutrients for itself? What if it wanted to take all of the water for itself? Before long, the huge tree would wither. If the entire tree dies, would a single root survive? No, it would not. The tree will only grow bigger if many of its roots absorb water and nutrients. As the tree grows, you who are part of the tree will become even more aware of your mission, be filled with more energy, and be happier.

When thinking about human perfection, please remember this metaphor. Do not forget that the souls of all of humanity—not only humanity but also animals and plants—are part of this gigantic tree of life when viewed from the perspective of the great universe. From the perspective of the third dimension, all forms of life may seem separate and independent. They may seem different, in the same way that each root or leaf of a tree can appear distinct. But from a grander, spiritual perspective, they are all part of one huge tree. Say that human beings are the roots, then the plants could be the leaves and the animals could be the fruit or the bark of the tree. In this way, all living beings make up different parts of the tree.

All forms of life that exist in this great universe are there to sustain the life of this one huge tree of life. We must not forget this. We exist to keep this tree of life alive. The tree itself is growing by absorbing water and nutrients, and by going through transpiration and photosynthesis, or carbon assimilation. In the process, some leaves may wilt and fall off. Sometimes, the fruit may be spoiled by insects or the trunk may get damaged. The branches may be used to create a bird's nest, or parts of the roots may wither or be severed. Many things can happen. These things are what we perceive in this world as accidents or misfortune. However, we must not forget that despite these negative aspects, the tree is still trying to live as a whole.

4
The Three Points for Walking the Way to Human Perfection

Now that you have an understanding of what humans are through this metaphor, what should you do next? Please think about this. You are one of the roots and an extremely important part of the gigantic tree of life. However, no matter how big a tree may be, it will die if it does not have roots. Roots are very important; in fact, they are what supports the growth of a tree.

With this in mind, let me tell you about three important things that you must do.

(1) Awaken to the great mission

First, you must tell yourself that you will *not* gain any benefit by fulfilling your true mission. Just as roots absorb water and nutrients and send them up a tree, we humans are serving a higher purpose. Although you may appear to gain some benefits, they only stay with you for a while and are not yours to keep. You cannot keep the benefits or wonderful things to yourself. This is the thing you must understand as a given. The benefits may remain with you temporarily or pass through you for a period of time, but if you try to keep them for yourself, the tree of life will die. You must know this. If you think that the benefits are yours and try to keep them from others or block these benefits from passing, the gigantic tree of life will wither. This is the first point.

Perhaps you have heard of the place called hell. By now, you should be able to imagine what it really is. We are essentially part of the great tree of life and our purpose is to serve the tree as its roots. However, there are people among us who begin to hold mistaken ideas. These people claim that roots have freedom and try to absorb more water and nutrients for themselves. Having forgotten their original mission and role, they begin to think selfishly and try to hoard the water and nutrients they have absorbed.

What happens as a result? They probably do not know. Just look at the tree trunk high above you. Look at the branches and the leaves. They are withering. The flowers are dying and the fruit is rotting. The tree has stopped forming growth rings. Can't you see? Guiding spirits are always teaching us this, but the roots underground think they have nothing to do with it because they cannot see what is above ground. Having forgotten their original mission, they think that it is none of their business and try to keep all of the water and nutrients for themselves.

Even if you try to keep the water and nutrients to yourself, it makes no difference because the same amount will always be in front of you even if you let it flow. This fact does not change, but when you forget your mission, a serious death awaits you. It means the tree of life itself will die. Here lies the reason for hell to form. Because each root only thinks about itself and about life underground, those above ground suffer, weaken, and die. That is why, in every age, those with great character known as guiding spirits are born on earth to teach the true Laws. They give true teachings. They teach the Laws, many, many times and do not stop until their lives end. They never stop teaching the Laws, even if it entails the danger of getting crucified like Jesus. They never stop teaching the truth because they know that if they stop, it will lead to the huge tree of life, which spans the whole universe, to wither. Guiding spirits teach us our mission because they are aware of such danger. "Do not be selfish. Love others." "Love your neighbor." "Do not live only for yourself." They always teach us these lessons. Do not forget them. You must never forget them. This is the first point for you to follow.

To put it differently, you must awaken to your great mission. But this sense of mission is nothing new. You have had it from the very beginning. You have simply forgotten the mission you originally had. So you must realize how much is expected of you in this lifetime. To awaken to your new mission and to awaken to the mission you originally had are the same thing. But think about how urgent and crucial it is for people today to realize and act on this. This is the first point.

(2) Unleash your true power

There is the second point. The second point is that simply doing your job is not enough. I said that the roots have a mission to absorb water and nutrients and send them up the tree. But, is that all you have to do? Do you just need to let them flow?

There is an old Chaplin film called *Modern Times*. It depicts a man whose job is simply to tighten the nuts on bolts that are transported on a conveyor belt. The film depicts him comically. We often tend to be buried in simple, repetitive tasks like this. Each day passes mundanely, and we do not think twice about it. What is more, we end up setting our own limits. We tend to tell ourselves, "This is how I am," or "I'm just a root, so this is the best I can do."

But at that time, you must consider whether there is more work you can do. Rather than being a small root like a capillary, why not grow bigger so you can contribute more? You could even become large enough to support the entire tree. You should seriously ask yourself whether you have that possibility. What do you think? Is it possible for you to grow large like that?

The answer is, yes. I believe human beings have great potential. I have always said that people's abilities in regard to office work can vary by as much as tenfold. But in work that affects people's minds, a person can achieve 100 or 1,000 times more, or even 10,000 times or more, after they awaken to their mission and make an all-out effort. When a person awakens, they will have a million times more power. This is indeed true. They truly have such power.

How much work will you be able to do when you become awakened? The amount will not be equal to the work of a single person. Work that affects people's minds has a strong power of influence and power of transmission, so you can accomplish far greater work than you can imagine.

In the past few years, I have already given lectures to over 50,000 people. I have reached millions including those who have listened to my recordings or read my books. This would not have been possible if I had been living an ordinary life. I could do all of this because I awakened to my mission and strongly believed that I must fulfill it. I am not making efforts for myself. Having awakened to my mission, I believed that I had to keep sending "water" and "nutrients" to more people. That is why I have kept making efforts. And because of that, I have been able to convey my messages to millions of people in just a few years. Actually, they are not *my* messages; they are the strong passion that comes from a far-distant world. I have succeeded in conveying this passion.

Over 1,000 people are here today, but to me, this is a very small gathering. The audience I see in front of me is much larger. I am not here to speak to an audience of just over 1,000 people; I am speaking to the millions of people living in Hokkaido. That is because I believe that you, who are listening to my lecture today, will surely convey my passion to others. This is the only time I will speak here this year, so I am speaking as if I am talking to millions of people. So my audience is not just 1,000 or so people.

This is the true nature of spiritual work—work that affects people's minds. The ability of one person may be limited, but once their work turns into spiritual work and gains momentum, it will have boundless influence. The burning of just one blade of dry grass is not a big fire. But if one blade catches fire and it spreads to other grass, it will gain tremendous power. In this way, even the flame of a single blade of dry grass can change the fate of an entire country. You may see yourself as a small blade of dry grass, but if a fire is lit on this single blade, it will never stop or be extinguished. Its energy will keep on increasing without limit. Never ever forget this.

So, here is the second point I want to make today on the way to human perfection. You must know that there is no limit to the spiritual work you can do. There may be a limit to worldly work. However, once you awaken to your mission, your work becomes limitless. In terms of time, your work will keep exerting power for hundreds or thousands of years, or even longer. In terms of space, it will go beyond Japan and spread across the world. This is a wonderful fact. You must know this. So, as the second point of human perfection, you must unleash your true power at all costs; your only choice is to unleash it.

(3) Accumulate wisdom day by day

Next, there is a third point I want to make. When your spiritual energy is unleashed, it will spread like wildfire, but in the midst of this passion, you must remain wise.

Passion is a great energy on earth. Actually, it is the *only* energy to accomplish great work on earth. Passion is the energy and wisdom is there to make this passion more wonderful and elevated. When your passion spreads, you will experience many things along the way. You will gain many experiences you have never had before. These experiences will give power to your knowledge. Knowledge empowered by experience is called wisdom.

You probably have much knowledge already. You may have gained it by reading books, listening to other people, or studying at school. And your knowledge probably continues to increase day by day. But knowledge alone has no power. Please remember this. Knowledge is no more than raw material. Of course, in order to gain power, you constantly need to acquire raw material. Even so, it is merely raw material. What gives power to this raw material is passion and the experience gained with this passion. Knowledge becomes wisdom when it is combined with passion. So here, now, please cherish wisdom. This means you must strive to be someone with much greater wisdom, all the more so this year than last year. Next year, you must possess much greater wisdom than you do this year.

Having wisdom means you are capable of guiding many people in the right direction. You will not have this kind of power with knowledge or passion alone. Passion is like a fire that spreads wildly without any specific direction. It can spread in ways you do not expect. But when wisdom is added, this flame of passion will start to work as it should. It will do marvelous work. It will start working constructively and positively and will improve this world in a tangible way.

So you must accumulate wisdom day by day. Wisdom is your treasure. Wisdom never comes to you just by reading books. It will not come just by listening to others. However, you can gain raw material this way. That raw material will turn into gold if you put it through a fire. It will then become solid gold. Therefore, from this year on, or rather, from this day on, absorb knowledge of the Truth and take action with passion. By combining knowledge and action, or knowledge and experience, you must keep producing unique, magnificent, jewel-like wisdom.

Wisdom, in turn, will allow you to accomplish great work. This is similar to the way a large cogwheel works. Without wisdom, we can only exert energy in one direction. But look at large machines. They have various gears to transmit power in all directions—right or left, up or down. This is how work is truly done. Passion alone does not point in a particular direction, or perhaps it may only know how to go straight. But when wisdom is added to passion, it can exert influence in many different fields, just as gears direct power in many different directions.

The Exploration of Right Mind

To sum up, there are three basic principles for walking the way to human perfection. The first principle is that there is nothing you can keep for yourself alone. You must understand that you exist to serve a greater mission. The second is that the spiritual work you can achieve with the power of passion is limitless. The third is that when the gear called wisdom gives direction to the unlimited power called passion, you can perform work at even higher levels. These are the starting points and the basic attitudes.

However, these things are also not enough to walk the way to human perfection. There is one more thing I want you to practice as you constantly check the three points I mentioned. That is the exploration of your mind.

Human beings have a mind. Actually, it is not accurate to say that humans have a mind; it is no mistake to say that the mind is the only thing there is. When you die, you can only bring your mind back to the other world. That is the only thing you can bring with you. You will not be able to bring your glasses, shirt, or tie. The mind is all you can take. So improving the mind is the only mission or spiritual discipline for humans to focus on.

Therefore, in addition to your sense of mission, always remember to explore your mind. At Happy Science, we call it "The Exploration of Right Mind." It may not be very easy to know what righteousness is because exploring Right Mind means exploring God's Will. Because it is we, human beings, who are exploring God's Will, there is no uniformity or limit to the righteousness we are exploring. No matter how deeply we explore righteousness, we will never be able to fully understand it. But that is precisely why humans are on a road of eternal improvement.

So today, let me give you some advice on exploring Right Mind to become a great person. First, never hold negative thoughts. Some examples of negative thoughts include thoughts that harm others or harm yourself. They also include complaints, discontent, jealousy, and suspicion, among others. You can probably think of an endless number of them. Control your mind so you do not hold negative thoughts like this. This is the first aspect of Right Mind.

Second, if your negative thoughts have become strong enough that you express them through your mouth, hands, legs, or actions, reflect on them immediately. If mistaken thoughts manifest as actions, reflect on them right away. Make sure to never repeat the same deed or utter the same words. This is the second checkpoint. Strive not to have negative thoughts, but if you do, make it a habit to reflect on them right away.

Then, here is the third point I want to make. You cannot finish removing the dirt from your mind immediately or after just one or two attempts. You may assume a higher position, a higher status, or feel you have attained higher enlightenment, but your mind can still become clouded. So never forget to keep on cleaning the mirror of your mind every single day. Do not forget to constantly clean your mind. Your position, status, title, or the praise of others will never be a valid excuse not to do this.

I, too, clean the mirror of my mind every day. As soon as I notice that it is clouded, I reflect on myself. Today, I am talking about self-reflection in front of you, and last night, I spent over an hour reflecting on myself.

The higher your position, the stricter your self-reflection must be because there will be more things that can cloud your mirror. This is an eternal discipline. As long as we are human there is no end to it, for me and also for you. As we go through this eternal discipline, we are walking the way to perfection. Please never forget this. That is all for today's lecture. Thank you very much.

CHAPTER THREE

Love, Nurture, and Forgive

Consecutive Seminars in Kyushu, 1989

Originally recorded in Japanese on September 9, 1989
at Munakata Yurix in Fukuoka Prefecture, Japan
and later translated into English.

1
The Core Idea of My Philosophy

Today's lecture was supposed to be a seminar for Happy Science members, but given the size of the audience, it feels like a public lecture. Although a few hundred people in the audience are non-members, the content of today's seminar will be mainly for our members.

Happy Science has been a very welcoming group that would make you feel as if you were back home with your family from the beginning. It was and is a highly transparent group with much heart-to-heart communication. Even so, making progress has sometimes made things difficult for us; as we have grown larger, the amount of work we have needed to do has increased and more emphasis has been placed on efficiency and efficacy. Although I am not completely satisfied with the current situation, I am happy to see how, in local branch activities, the traditional culture of our group is being preserved. This makes me reflect deeply on how we must keep this warm atmosphere as we continue to carry out activities in Tokyo. In essence, warm feelings flow from one person's heart to another. I believe we must not lose sight of this to the end. I publish books and address people through writing, but in principle, our basic approach should be face-to-face communication. The best way to communicate is to talk directly to people.

For today's seminar, I chose the title, "Love, Nurture, and Forgive." This phrase is very dear to me and gives me courage. Whenever I return to the starting point of our activities, these words always come to mind.

Almost nine years ago, I was living in a completely different environment than I am in now. Back then, I never imagined I would be doing the kind of work I do currently. One day, I suddenly started receiving messages from a world beyond this one, from a world of another dimension. This experience was real; it came to me like a bolt from the blue. Later on, as I read various books, I learned that other people had also experienced such an event. For example, Tadao Yanaihara, who served as the president of the University of Tokyo, had an experience similar to mine. Right before he entered the University of Tokyo, he was suddenly drawn to Christianity and became deeply immersed in it. Another example is Mother Teresa, who is known as the holy mother of India. One day, while she was on the train, she heard the voice of Jesus and awakened to her mission. That was how she decided to start her activities. I knew that such things were depicted in books or had happened in the past, and I had no doubts about them. When they actually happened to me, however,

I had no idea how to understand them. In fact, I was not ready for this kind of event.

Therefore, I was truly astounded when I received my first spiritual revelation. At that time, I did not have any writing paper but only index cards at hand. I picked one up, anticipating that something was about to happen. I held a pencil and waited. Then, my hand suddenly began moving on its own. It clearly was not of my own will. On the first card, my hand wrote *iishirase*, in Japanese katakana characters, which means "Good News." I picked up another card, and my hand wrote "Good News" again, then again on the third card and many more after that. So I said, "I got that. Do you have any other messages?" Then my hand wrote "Good News" again and that was all for that day. Still, I had a strong hunch that many things would happen to me from then on. For about a week, I received spiritual communication but did not know how to understand it. But gradually, I got used to the spiritual phenomena and started to have conversations with beings who were not of this world.

The very first teaching that I received during that time was, as is today's title, "Love, Nurture, and Forgive." I was told that this was the first teaching. After that, I contemplated the meaning of the phrase for months. I understood that the single phrase, "Love, Nurture, and Forgive," would be my work in this life and that it would be the core idea of the many philosophies I would put out from then on.

I kept contemplating this single phrase for nearly three years. During that time, I continued to experience various spiritual phenomena. While working at a trading company, I repeated to myself, "Love, Nurture, and Forgive" again and again. I wondered, "What can I do about this? What is expected of me?" It was like a Zen dialogue without any explanation of the phrase. I was simply told that it was my job to figure out how to understand and practice those words. I did not know what I could do at that time given the position, work, and environment I was in, but I kept contemplating the idea while putting it into practice.

Then, when I was around 27 years old, I put forth the theory of the developmental stages of love, which came out of this single phrase. Three years of contemplation led me to the idea that love has developmental stages. I wrote about this philosophy in one of my core books, *The Laws of the Sun*. With the completion of this philosophy, I entered the second phase of exploring the phrase, "Love, Nurture, and Forgive." After taking three years to develop the theory of the developmental stages of love, it took me another three years to be ready to stand before you. During those years, I kept contemplating this key phrase, about the thoughts and actions that this idea would give rise to.

2

From "Taking Love" to "Giving Love"

My realization that I was seeking the wrong type of happiness

The more I contemplated these three concepts, the more I realized that they pointed in a specific direction. All three concepts of "love," "nurture," and "forgive" indicate a proactive approach to others and say absolutely nothing about what you will gain in return. In other words, they are teachings of altruism.

However, when I received this message nine years ago, at the age of 24, I had completely the opposite attitude. I was seeking to be loved, nurtured, and forgiven by others. I wanted to be loved by others. I wanted others to be kind to me, to praise me, and to admire me. I was struggling to get these things, yet I was told to make a 180-degree change in my attitude and do the opposite. I wondered whether that would bring me any benefit. I thought, "I'm told I must forgive others, but look at the world. It's full of contradictions, wrong and upsetting things, so how can I possibly forgive these things?" I was full of moral indignation. "I must not let the world be as it is. I must condemn it somehow." This is what I believed. But the message I received was teaching me to do the complete opposite.

About six months before I received this message, I was very introspective and often reflected on my inner self. Looking back, there were two major problems that troubled me the most during those times. One was the matter of my own self-realization. I had a strong wish to develop my abilities and open up the way to the life I aspired to live. Although I aimed to be the ideal version of myself, the reality was not what I wanted. No matter how much effort I put in, things did not work out and I was led to a different path.

The other problem was, like I said, the issue of love. Adults who have had a very usual upbringing will naturally feel happy when they are loved. That is natural. You may think so, too. In adolescence, however, we often have the opposite experience and suffer for not being able to get the love that we seek. If I analyze the state of mind I had back then, I must admit that I had the opposite attitude to what I now teach at Happy Science. I had a tendency to minimize what people had given to me. On the other hand, I had a strong feeling of disappointment when I did not get what I wanted or when I was not treated how I wanted to be. When this happened, I became regretful, frustrated, anguished, and unhappy, and I thought it was natural to feel that way.

Ever since I was around 10 years old, I liked to write poetry and have written many. People who write poems tend to have a very sensitive personality. It is good if they are sensitive to good things, but in most cases, it is the opposite; they are most probably sensitive to bad things. When they sense bad things and feel hurt, they let out their "pus-like feelings" in the form of prose or poetry, and doing so makes them feel refreshed. I had the tendency to do that myself as well. When people praised me, I could not accept their praise as it was, and when they slandered or criticized me, their words pierced me like thorns. They would be stuck in me for two or three years, or sometimes even longer. That was my situation.

Looking back, I now understand that even though people say many things in all kinds of situations, they do not necessarily say them out of ill will. They are just saying things casually or thoughtlessly with no sense of responsibility whatsoever. Even so, some of these words can pierce others' hearts and make them suffer for years. We often do this ourselves, so we can assume that others will do the same. I could have realized this back then, but I did not.

Back then, I was deeply disappointed with myself. I was feeling very miserable and felt worthless. I wondered, "Why was I given life in this world?" "If I can only live in a clumsy way like this, why was I born in the first place?" I would bemoan deeply like this.

However, after encountering the phrase, "Love, Nurture, and Forgive," I gradually realized that the happiness I was seeking was wrong. I used to think that happiness meant receiving something from others. To be specific, I was happy when I was praised or admired by others. I was happy when I did something that I felt deserved other people's praise. That was how I felt. But the direction indicated by the three concepts of "Love, Nurture, and Forgive" was not like that at all.

List the love you gave and the love you received

I looked back and pondered, "Have I ever done things for others with love? Have I even thought about loving others to begin with?" However, I could hardly remember thinking and doing this. On the contrary, the more I thought about it, the more I realized how much others had done for me. Of course, the love from my mother and father came to mind first. I also remembered the many favors from other people, including my friends and teachers. The only thing I could think of that I had done for them was that I studied hard to meet their expectations while they supported me and provided me with a good learning environment. But I had done so only to gain recognition and to satisfy myself, or to feel happy by becoming greater as a person. This is what I realized.

So I drew what we call the "balance sheet of love" in Happy Science. I put the "love I had given" on one side of a piece of paper and the "love others had given me" on the other side. When I tried to list them in my mind, I struggled to recall the love I had given to others. I could only find a few examples of what I had done to make someone else happy. On the other hand, I could make an endless list of what others had done for me. To do something for others is a good thing; it is a plus. What others had done for me would be a "debt" or a minus because I had taken from them. When I compared my pluses and minuses on the balance sheet, I realized I would have deep regrets if I died the way I was living.

I had never looked at things in that way before then. For example, when I studied hard, got good marks, and received praise, I felt I was a great person. When I became the center of attention, I thought my life was fulfilled and complete. That was how I felt then, but when I changed my perspective, I realized what a terrible life I had been living.

Come to think of it, five billion people are living on earth (as of the lecture) and over 100 million are living in Japan. What if each of these people were to write their own balance sheet of love, listing the things they had done for others and things others had done for them? If they had hardly done anything for others and only received favors, then the people on earth would be a massive group of debtors. This would be what the world we live in would be like. It would mean they are no different from "vampires" taking love from many others.

Speaking of vampires, there are slimy blood-sucking creatures called leeches in rice fields. They stick to your legs and suck your blood, which is really loathsome. We find them loathsome because they just suck our blood without doing anything productive. They give us pain and grow fat themselves, which is truly horrible. The same is true for mosquitoes. They sneak up and steal our blood, which we worked hard to make by eating food. It may be OK if they paid us [*laughs*], but they don't. They sneak up, steal from us, and disappear before you know it. You will be left with an unpleasant feeling. That is a shared feeling that humans have. I am sure there are people who act like leeches and mosquitoes, but those people, who do not produce anything but just take what others have worked hard to create, are naturally disliked.

You may think, "Why can't I get more love, admiration, or praise?" "Why is this all I get?" But if you solely focus on getting or receiving something, just as a mosquito or leech does, then you will certainly be disliked. It is a natural consequence, so it is wrong for you to complain about it. By now, you should understand why you were not given love. Even nice people will not allow mosquitoes to suck their blood. That is right; people who are like mosquitoes will be disliked. Or, at the very least, they will not be given what they want.

Examine whether you are expecting something in return

During adolescence, relationship issues can arise in addition to issues of love in general. This is a time in our lives when we seek the love of the opposite sex the most. You may agonize over not being loved, but have you ever thought about how much you have done for the person you love? You may realize you have not thought about it deeply. Even if you did something for the person, did you expect a favor in return? You may have thought, "I did this for them so I deserve a reward. But I received nothing. That's not fair. I'm sad and frustrated."

I am sure that even among you, there are some who believe they are giving love but are actually doing it to receive something in return. If you do not receive anything at the time, your "love" will immediately turn into suffering.

That is because your love is not true love. Love that expects something in return is not true love. You can understand this better by imagining yourself giving someone a gift. There is nothing wonderful about giving a gift to someone if you are doing it to get something in return. You are giving a gift because you want to express your gratitude to that person. Sometimes, you may receive something in return, but usually, people do not give a gift for the sake of getting something in return. You would most likely think that people who do are quite odd. You may be able to understand this in the context of gift-giving, but when it comes to your mental attitude, it becomes a completely different story; you tend to have the opposite way of thinking and usually want to receive something in return.

Now, I want to ask the more than 1,000 people here to reflect on your life. Compare the things you did for others and the things others did for you. I believe that having an equal amount on both sides is the minimum condition for being a human. If you were given more, it means you have been living your life in debt and have been a burden on many people.

You will be happy by benefiting many people

What we have been given from others is immense, indeed. However, what we give back to them is very little. When I realized this, I changed my way of thinking. I used to think that happiness was to achieve what I wanted to accomplish or to obtain things that could be listed on paper. I thought that fulfilling these wishes was my happiness. But I realized there was a far bigger happiness.

People feel happy when they have a strong presence, or in other words when they feel they are developing and becoming more important. Their wish to be recognized is the same as their desire to develop themselves. But if you wish to truly develop yourself, you cannot do so by trying to take from others. That is because taking is merely an effort to cover up your shortcomings. The true meaning of self-expansion is to sow seeds or a part of your soul, spirit, or mind into other people. It means to inspire others with your ways of living and thinking. This is what is truly important.

People generally think, "To give is to lose, and to receive is to gain." But in the world of the mind, the more you give, the more you develop. For example, speaking in front of 1,500 people is one form of self-development for me. I can talk to 1,500 of you here and have a positive influence on your ways of thinking. I can add something good to your lives. In this way, I can develop myself much more than just adding something to my own life.

If you truly want to develop yourself, you must not try to protect yourself. You can only gain a small sense of satisfaction by protecting yourself. True happiness is the sense of self-expansion and self-development that you feel based on the belief that you are infinitely useful and helpful. So, you will naturally be happy by becoming someone who can truly benefit many people. That is what it means to be an "egoist" in the truest sense. You must understand it that way. Everyone is too satisfied with being their small self. If you really want to benefit yourself, you must change your perspective. I came to realize this. This was the basic approach I took.

3

What Does It Mean to Love Others?

By aspiring to give love, your life will start to change

To love others is easy to say but difficult to practice. I would like you to think about it. It is indeed very difficult to practice giving love. What pops into your mind when you think of giving love? Is it to offer your seat on a crowded train or to help a small child who fell down to get back up? These kinds of actions may quickly come to mind. But what if you were asked to describe what it means to nurture others in your everyday life? This is a very difficult question to answer. It is very difficult, indeed. You will not find any book that covers these topics. There are no books that give you a list of examples of what it means to love others or to nurture others. This is something you must discover for yourself.

If you are married, for example, you may believe you love your spouse. But is your love toward your spouse the same as the love I am talking about? Please think about it. You may find that they do not match. You may believe that you have been showering your spouse with love, but there may be a problem with your love from two perspectives. First, you may have accepted as a matter of course that you will receive something in return for devoting yourself to your spouse. Second, you may believe you are giving love when in fact you are just trying to bind your spouse. You may have put a limit on his or her thoughts and deeds in the name of love. Perhaps you are realizing this now. These are some things you will not realize unless someone tells you.

The same is true of parental love. Some parents say they love their children when in fact they are only making a habit of worrying about their children. What are they worrying about? If you listen to the words they speak, you will find that they often say, "My child might be involved in an accident," "He may fail the exam," or "She may become a delinquent." They always assume that bad things will happen and confuse "worry" for "love." Many parents are like this. Do they truly worry for the sake of their children? It may not necessarily be the case. Please think deeply about this. Are you worried for your own sake? Are you worried because *you* do not want any trouble? Perhaps you are always fearful about what *you* do not want to happen.

Take, for example, parents whose child is planning to take an entrance exam. They worry that their child might fail the exam, but are they really thinking about their child's future? It may be that they are worried about what others might say about them if their child fails. They may be worried about the extra burden or anxiety they will have to live with for another year. There are many cases like this. Have you ever expressed your love out of much purer intentions, truly for the benefit of other people? If you think in this way, you will understand how difficult it is to give love, even though it is the idea that lies at the starting point of Happy Science. Indeed, it is difficult. It is not so easy to practice it.

But everything starts with knowing. You must know that giving love is one of the objectives of our spiritual discipline. You must also know that by aspiring to give love, your life will start to change. Knowing these things is the starting point and the first step.

I experienced for myself that this idea is true and right. Before encountering this key phrase, I used to seek admiration, praise, respect, and kindness from others. But I decided to stop seeking these things and instead desired to help others and do things that would make them happy. I made up my mind to do things that would make others smile, and the moment I began to live that way, my life started to change. Now, I no longer desire praise from others. I do not need admiration or appreciation from others. When I made up my mind to live for many people and took one step, then two, a completely different view unfolded before my eyes. Many people came to support me. Many people emerged to support my idea. It was truly surprising. If you try to live for your own sake, others will not help you, but if you try to live for others, you will receive help. This surprising paradox occurred. It is truly a curious occurrence but I have no doubt that it is the way the world works.

The love you gave will be yours

Let me delve further into this topic of love. In our Happy Science books, you may have often read that "love that gives" is another name for "unconditional love." Our books say that simply giving love is important, and that love dies when you expect something in return. The phrase, "Love dies when you expect something in return," is poetic, but I am not saying this just for the beautiful sound of the words. The phrase states the truth.

You may try to do something good for others. However, if you do so expecting an equal or greater reward, your good deed will be canceled out. I say that you must not expect anything in return because, when you do not, the love you gave will be yours. In fact, this is a great law that applies to all human minds. It is essential to know this single truth while living on earth. The love you gave will be yours. This is the law. It is the law in the world of the unseen.

You have probably read about the lives of many great figures. Why are they considered great? It is because they gave many things. Even though they did not expect anything in return, what they gave became theirs. To explain this in terms of the "physics of God's Light" or the law of physics in the Spirit World, one's light increases in proportion to the amount of love they have given.

In your mind, you may have a pure wish to help someone. Viewed spiritually, the moment you emit such thoughts or take such actions, a halo is emitted from the back of your head. The halo is given to you from the heavenly world. The light is cast from above. The moment you think or act out of a pure wish for others, light is emitted. You may not be able to see this light, but it is surely emitted. As proof, think about the feeling you get when you do something to make others truly happy from your heart. Do you feel warmth in your heart? Others may feel the warmth, but you, too, will feel it. Even in the middle of winter, you will feel warm inside. This is proof that you are shedding light. With spiritual sight, you can see even in a mirror that you are emitting light. A halo is formed behind your head when you have good thoughts or are full of love for others. When you are thinking of giving, you are also being given.

This truth is deeply connected to the reason God created human beings. We have learned that human beings are children of God. This means that we carry within us the same nature as God. What is that nature? God has many attributes, but you all know that, essentially, God is love. You know that God is love, indeed. God is love, so as children of God, we are closest to our true selves when we give love to others. At that time, you can truly recognize yourself as a child of God. At that time, you are given God's Light as if to prove that you are a child of God, and you emit a halo.

The halo may just be temporary, but those who live with loving thoughts every day are always surrounded by people with smiles. They are always filled with light. You may have had an experience where a room suddenly felt brighter when a particular person walked in. People like that emit a strong halo or aura. These people are always filled with a wish to make others happy, so they brighten up the room when they enter it. They make it a habit to keep positive thoughts in their minds, and their habit becomes the ability to light up the space around them and shows up as a phenomenon.

In Buddhism, Shakyamuni Buddha often taught about the merit of offering. Why is it important to make offerings? This was not taught for the sake of monks. Buddhist monks were poor because they did not have secular jobs, but they did not necessarily walk around teaching people the merit of offering and collecting alms just to satisfy their hunger. The act of making an offering is important because the love and virtue you put into the offering will become your own. They will belong to the person who makes the offering. That was why Buddha taught the importance of making offerings.

Shakyamuni Buddha always taught his disciples, "Although you may appear like beggars, be confident when accepting alms. You are not beggars. You are actually giving. By giving people the opportunity to make an offering, you are giving them great love. You are teaching them the most important mindset as a human. Teachings are not only given through the mouth. Teachings are not only learned through the ears. Teachings can be found in usual behaviors and everyday events. You do not need to speak any words. Just hold out your bowl. At that time, teach and guide them without words. That is what is important. Teach them how lighthearted, precious, and happy they can become through their acts of giving. You must guide them to awaken to these feelings just by holding out your bowl."

Buddha always preached, "You are not begging but instead giving people a great revelation. You are giving them a chance to make contact with the Great Light. So you must not deprecate yourselves. Do not belittle yourselves for receiving alms. You are giving others a precious chance to attain enlightenment. Engrave this firmly in your minds and collect alms every day knowing that it will lead you and others to great enlightenment. This is a way to enlighten people and to draw them closer to the Truth." Buddha often taught his disciples in this way. He was right, indeed.

When placing an offering of food or drink in a monk's bowl, some people may wish, "Please allow me to go back to heaven after death" or "Please erase all of my sins." If they have such thoughts, however, the value of their offering will be reduced to nothing. What you give will be yours, but the moment you expect a reward, the virtue you gained from giving disappears. Spiritually, you will gain nothing.

I have heard that many people have now awakened to the Truth and risen to spread the Light of the Truth. I imagine many of you are doing volunteer work in many ways. At that time, remember that your earnest desire to help others is valuable in and of itself. When you aspire to help others and take action, the virtue that comes with it will be yours. The love you give will be yours. It will belong to you. So never remind yourself of how much you did. Do not ever think in such a way. Do not try to win recognition for what you did.

When you practice an act of love, forget about it. You must not count your achievements and remember what you did. Or worse, if you complain about not getting enough in return or enough admiration, it means you have not made any progress as a seeker of the Truth. It may even mean you have regressed. Please bear this in mind. Even if you have had good thoughts and done good deeds, forget about them.

Love must be a feeling that naturally arises in you. You do what you do because you feel like doing it or because it makes you happy. This attitude is important. Your actions, speech, and thoughts must come out naturally. They must come out because it is normal for you to do so or because you like to do so out of your nature. You do not need to let others know of what you did. If you do, your virtue will be gone. Others do not need to know. Just forget about it. Instead, make an effort to remember what others have done for you, although this is a difficult thing to do. We tend to remember what we did for others and forget what others did for us. That is why we do not hear many words of gratitude in this world. So try to remember what others did for you and forget what you did for others. Even if you are not rewarded, the person you gave love to will surely feel happy. This happiness will then give rise to further thoughts and deeds that bring happiness. When a person is loved, they will not be able to keep it to themselves. They will surely want to do something for others.

Think about it. You may not see it or hear it, but the love you give will do more work on its own. When you give love to someone, he or she will then do an act of love for someone you do not know at all. Love will be passed on in this way. That is love. Love works on its own. That is what makes us happy. That is why we feel joy. Please remember this. I strongly hope so.

My teachings come down to "love that gives"

The first concept in my teachings is to love others, or "love that gives." Everything boils down to this single point. I give many teachings at Happy Science, but everything comes down to love. I teach the Principle of Happiness: Love, Wisdom, Self-Reflection, and Progress, but they are all for the sake of love.

What is the purpose of wisdom? Wisdom is there for you to love more and more people. By knowing more, you can benefit more people. You will not be able to help others if you only have little knowledge or intellectual power. By learning more, you can expand the range of your activities. You will be able to have a greater influence on others. That is why wisdom is important. Wisdom supports love.

I also teach self-reflection. Why is this important? It is because the act of giving love that you think you are doing may not, in actual fact, truly accord with God's Will. That is why you need to examine yourself in relation to this point. Many people believe they are doing good when in fact they are going astray. Many try hard to justify themselves by boasting about their good deeds. Some become too kind to others and end up spoiling them. Some do good because they want to be praised. These people have forgotten their pure motives and are craving recognition from others.

As you may have noticed, although people have pure and healthy thoughts in the beginning, they tend to forget them and go astray as they practice love. That is the nature of ordinary people. So we need to correct ourselves and that is why we need self-reflection. Thus, self-reflection is needed for love.

In addition, there is the teaching of progress. Progress, too, is there for love. How will love be expressed when it gains power? When the power of love gets stronger, love will surely spread among many people. It means you will want to help as many people as possible. You will wish for more and more people to be filled with smiles and joy. So progress simply means the expansion of love. It is the process of love growing bigger. That is the nature of progress. It is the growth of the ideal of love.

To sum up, although some may find it difficult to understand the Fourfold Path, it all comes back to love. Wisdom, self-reflection, and progress are there to make love stronger, bigger, and more wonderful. Please understand this.

Let me also talk about the Exploration of Right Mind, which is the basic guideline of Happy Science. This is a kind of discipline. To use an old terminology, it may be called a "precept." If you wish to study the Truth at Happy Science and polish your mind, you must always explore Right Mind as a precept. What this means is that you need a basic attitude when aspiring to do good and take action. The Exploration of Right Mind will shape this basic attitude.

In fact, the act of giving love is what God Himself wishes to do. Giving love is the work we do on behalf of God or as part of God. This is the most precious work that we must prioritize over everything else. We have been assigned this important mission. So we must reflect on ourselves daily and make sure we do not have wrong thoughts or do bad deeds. This is our sacred duty. If we are to carry out a mission as part of God, we must do it properly and we must constantly remind ourselves of that. To this end, we need to explore Right Mind as a precept. Please understand it in this way.

You are giving away a free bouquet called "love"; you are giving out a flower to each person. Although this work seems easy to do, you need to be qualified to do this. If you do it with the wrong mind, the flowers will no longer be free gifts because you will not provide a refreshing feeling to the people who receive them. That is why you always need to explore Right Mind.

4

The Requirements for "Nurturing Others"

Now, I would like to talk about nurturing people. It is very difficult to nurture people. There is no end to this pursuit. You can guide a person or be kind to someone on a one-on-one basis if you make an effort, but in terms of your ability to guide many people, there is no limit to how much you can improve. No matter how capable you may be, it is not easy to guide many people. This is true for all human beings.

There are two elements that are absolutely necessary to practice "nurturing love" or to nurture other people. One is intellect or knowledge. You need to be smart, or in other words, be able to think well about various matters. To be able to think about how someone can become a better person, you need to have food for thought and also be able to see the cause and effect that comes with using it. For example, you must be able to discern, "He will turn out to be like this if I do this," "She will respond like this if I teach this," or "This effort will result in this." Unless you can see this chain of cause and effect, you will not be able to guide people in the right way. So what we mean by "knowledge" or "intellect" at Happy Science is the ability to see the chain of cause and effect. It is important to know what kind of fruit different seeds will bear. This ability can be gained through reading books or by obtaining information from various sources.

Another indispensable element is experience. People can learn from experience. Of course, experience can often come from the repetition of trial and error. In the beginning, we fail many times and learn that a particular method does not work. However, there are patterns to how humans think and act, and the number of these patterns is limited. By accumulating experiences one by one, you will understand how people act in particular situations. So you can gain the ability to guide people by accumulating experiences. When you see someone facing a similar event that you failed in before, you can warn them about a possible downfall or failure.

Knowledge and experience are the two wheels of "nurturing love." You need to raise your intellect and deepen your experience; both are necessary. The types of people whose role is to instruct and guide many people could be company executives, leaders, or teachers. To hold a position like this, you must fulfill two conditions; one is to have knowledge by educating or cultivating yourself and the other is to have a stock of experiences.

Apart from this, what may also help you is to have an adviser whose knowledge and experience you can draw on. Having an adviser close by is a third option. If you lack knowledge and experience, you need to get help from people who have these things. But first, you need to be a person whom they would want to help even though you, yourself, do not have enough knowledge or experience. To be such a person, you essentially need open-heartedness and humility, or in other words, an attitude of being willing to learn from others at the basis. You can guide others by receiving help from advisers in this way.

These elements are essential for practicing nurturing love. So, while you can practice "fundamental love" starting today, it takes time and training to practice "nurturing love." Please remember that it takes effort. And by putting in the effort, you can take your nurturing love to much higher levels. That is what I want to say. There is no end to these efforts.

Currently, we strongly encourage Happy Science members to study the Truth because you need to know a lot to advance from practicing fundamental love to practicing nurturing love. There is a limit to what you can experience in life. It is not easy to gain many experiences and it takes a lot of time to do that, but the Truth teaches about it briefly and in a simple manner. Therefore, by mastering the Truth, you can gain years' or decades' worth of experience. Then, you can become an even greater missionary of love. This is what I am teaching.

5
Reaching the State of "Forgiving Others"

Above this is the teaching of forgiving others. This love is difficult to practice. It is very difficult, indeed. To be able to forgive others, your soul needs to go through enough hardship. Competent people can learn to guide and nurture others, but it is not easy to develop the capabilities to forgive others. These capabilities cannot be developed overnight. You probably want to avoid suffering, hardship, sadness, and pain if you could. This is a natural feeling and everyone probably feels this way. But these things that appear to be negative can turn into something positive. This can happen when you are at the stage of forgiving others.

Some people are blessed with great gifts and abilities. But no matter how great a gift or ability they have, they cannot be truly strong unless they go through adversity, hardship, or difficulty. Just as heated iron is struck and put through water to be made into a sword, you need to go through difficulties to become a truly great, strong "sword." To forgive others, you need to go through many experiences of having risen out of hardships and pain. So even if you have made many mistakes in the past, you can turn them into positive experiences. The more mistaken thoughts you have had or mistaken actions you have done in the past, and the more serious they are, the more likely you are to become an even greater leader. I want to say so. To be able to forgive others, you must know people's sadness. You cannot forgive a person if you do not understand why he or she is suffering.

Justice distinguishes good from evil. Many people at the nurturing stage, before entering the forgiving stage, must learn about justice to be able to tell right from wrong. Leaders must teach people to abandon what is wrong and choose what is right. This effort is the way to become a leader. However, there is a higher perspective. There is also the need to embrace those in the process of spiritual discipline.

What if there was no great love to embrace those who fail, stumble, or fall in the process of undergoing spiritual discipline? If that were the case, we would not be able to believe that ultimately God created this world and the human mind. What if God only smiled on those who were successful and not on those who failed? Observing precepts is a good thing, but what if God loved only those who observe precepts and not those who break them or who make mistakes? If the ultimate God was such a being we would not be able to believe in this world itself.

We are learning to abandon evil and choose good on a small scale, and at the same time, we are sensing the presence of great love that embraces all on a large scale. Thanks to this love, we are allowed to be humans and continue to be humans. The light of angels are clearly teaching us to choose good. They teach us to choose what is right. They teach us to be closer to God. But as we know, there is a place called "hell" in the world beyond this one. There are evil spirits and satans in hell. They emerge on earth to delude people and make them suffer. Essentially, these spirits are "failures," so you may think that removing these failed souls would make the world much better. However, they exist and carry out their activities.

This means there is a great forgiveness that surpasses the world of good and evil. If you think of this as someone else's problem, you can probably stay indifferent, but try to think about it as your problem. Everyone makes mistakes as they live as a human. If only successful people were saved and people who failed were not, who knows how many times we would have ceased to be human? Even so, we are given another chance. This is a blessing. That is why we can summon our courage.

Although we may fail at something, we can try again. Because we know we are always given another chance, we can tell ourselves, "OK, let's give it another try." We must know that the state of forgiving is much greater. It is close to the heart of God. Before this stage, at the stage of nurturing others, you must know good and bad, or what is right. But when you go beyond this level, you will become aware of the great embracing love. Souls that reach this level have experienced many setbacks for hundreds or thousands of reincarnations. They may have seen the suffering and sadness of many people and they, too, probably have feelings that resonate with them. Only after going through such hardships will they find mercy welling up from within.

In general, love is thought to be equal and horizontal. On the other hand, mercy flows vertically from top to bottom. Mercy flows endlessly from the infinite heights to the infinite depths. That is right. Humans undergo spiritual discipline, and as they raise their spirituality, they will develop an overwhelming love. All the lessons they gained through numerous reincarnations in the past will be the power that lets the single great river of love flow. This is the Invincible Thinking that I often talk about. You can turn everything you experience in this world into something positive. This is true if, rather than thinking about life from the perspective of a few decades, you think of it from a much longer perspective.

Mercy is a heart that never ceases to love people. It continues to give, like a spring that never runs dry. Before reaching this state, you will probably go through many trials. But you need to feel grateful for having these opportunities. Remind yourself that your soul is being polished now. Even as you study the Truth and make an effort every day, there may be times when you face difficulties. You may ask yourself why you should suffer such difficulties. However, remember that you are being presented with a great opportunity.

Successful people can nurture others. But you need to go through both success and failure to be able to forgive others. Only when you have learned both will you become a person of great love who can forgive everyone. This is what God expects of us. We must never forget this. Thank you very much for coming today.

CHAPTER FOUR

Rediscovering the Eightfold Path

The Seventh Public Lecture of 1989

Originally recorded in Japanese on October 8, 1989
at Marugame Civic Hall in Kagawa Prefecture, Japan
and later translated into English.

1
Why We Need Self-Reflection

For today's lecture, I chose the title, "Rediscovering the Eightfold Path." But some of you may be thinking, "I know nothing about the Eightfold Path to begin with, so how can I rediscover it? Give us a lecture on the Eightfold Path first and come back later to give us this one."

The Eightfold Path has become old and outdated in today's society. I imagine very few people can name all eight paths. But before speaking on the Eightfold Path, I must talk about self-reflection. The Eightfold Path is a specialized method of self-reflection, so I must first talk about what self-reflection is and why it is necessary.

When you were young, you were probably told that self-reflection was important. Perhaps your parents told you to reflect on your mistakes. But now, it may have become a thing of the past. No one will probably tell you to self-reflect after becoming an adult. If someone did, you may be offended and talk back to them. If your colleague told you to reflect on yourself, you would probably get angry at them. Or if your parents told you to reflect on yourself even though you are a grown adult, you would probably react even more sharply and say, "I'm an adult. Don't treat me like a child."

In this way, self-reflection is a concept that is easy to accept as a child but hard to open-heartedly accept as an adult. Why is this? Have you ever thought about this? As a child, you were able to humbly reflect on your deeds because your teacher or parents were the ones who told you to reflect on yourself. They were in a position of authority so you could not go against them. As children, you could not fight against your parents, nor could you fight against your teacher as they could have prevented you from graduating. Because of the clear difference in position, you could not help but obey them. So I would like you to take this opportunity to think again about why, as an adult, you cannot humbly reflect on yourself.

When you think about it, you will realize that one of the reasons lies in your pride. You may feel that you are already a responsible adult and that this feeling prevents you from being humble. You may think, "I'm a working adult wearing a suit and a tie. I work and earn a salary every month. It's obvious that I'm independent." I do not think that having such feelings, in and of itself, is a bad thing. Growing up to be an independent adult is a process of perfecting oneself, so it is natural to develop self-confidence.

However, there is also something wrong here. You have forgotten something or left something behind. What is it? As you ponder this, you will gradually realize that you have lost sight of something great. You were able to humbly respect people who were greater or higher than you when you were young, but as you grew older, you began to feel proud of yourself and became reluctant to listen to other people's advice. That is because you became unable to admit that some people were greater than you.

As we often learn, it is true that human beings are all equal in essence. This awareness of equality is an important energy that sustains our democratic society in this modern age. But this is precisely why people tend to take a defiant attitude. People tend to think, "I'm an independent person. Each person is unique and has individual character, so we must value that uniqueness," or "Everyone is equal and has equal rights, which must be respected." This idea, itself, is not wrong. Democracy is actually built on this idea.

But here is the problem. If people then think, "This is why I don't need to listen to others," there is a leap of logic. People like that think of themselves as independent from other people and that other people are not their business. But there is something wrong with this way of thinking. Why? It is because it prevents them from perceiving the world and other people deeply enough and makes them conceited. They believe all people are equal and are striving to outdo each other. They feel as though everyone is in the same sword fight, but they cannot see the differences in people's abilities. However, as they accumulate experience in the working world, their "swords" may break or they may run out of "arrows," and be defeated or get beaten down. By experiencing setbacks, they will realize that they are not perfect. Having said that, some people still do not realize this, even after experiencing setbacks. These people will develop stronger egos that will only grow bigger.

Life usually comes with various setbacks. As I wrote in my book, *Invincible Thinking*, everyone experiences setbacks at least once or twice, or even more times in their life. They will not necessarily tell you, but people do experience setbacks. Those who boast about their successes are often hiding their failures. The best way to embrace setbacks in a truly positive light is to absorb all the lessons you can from your failures. You must then change your way of thinking so you can improve yourself further. This is the biggest benefit you can get from your setbacks. Another benefit is that you can learn modesty and kindness. People who have experienced failure often develop a negative way of thinking, but they have good traits of kindness and humility. You must learn to acquire these qualities.

Those who are naturally proud or have deceived themselves throughout their lives do not try to learn humbly from their failures. Instead, they try to distort the facts to their advantage. Their egos have become so big that they cannot accept their failures. Some people's egos are even bigger than the whole universe. There is the idea of "universe as self" when attaining enlightenment, but their case is different. Perhaps it could be called "ego as universe." Their egos are heavier than the Earth and will not succumb to the opinions of humankind. "Say what you want. Drop an atomic bomb, if you want. But I won't change how I think. If people say I'm wrong, then it means the world is in the hands of the devil." This is the kind of mentality they have.

Why do they think in this way? It is because they believe they are highly talented and very powerful. They just keep on insisting, "I'm strong. I've never been defeated. I've never lost in a fight or an argument." But if that were truly the case, why are they trying so hard to put up a front? If you look into their hearts, you will see that they are actually very weak and vulnerable. They are easily hurt, so they try hard to protect themselves out of fear. They pretend to be tough by wearing iron armor. But since you cannot imagine that these people have such a weak heart, when you interact with them you get hurt. You might think, "He's so weird. I never imagined there would be people like him who are so quick to pick on others." All kinds of difficulties arise when one's ego is inflated.

This all has to do with the fundamental way in which people feel happiness. In many cases, people are happiest when they feel they are growing and developing. This sense of expanding the ego cannot be completely denied. The desire to develop oneself comes with an impulse to be happy. This is true with plants, as well. For example, bamboo grows taller, and other plants grow and bloom because they, too, want to be happy. This is an expansion of the ego. All living things have this nature and we cannot get rid of it. If we did, flowers would not bloom and trees would not bear fruit. Likewise, humans would not grow up or achieve success. So we cannot completely deny this nature that we all have.

Then, what should we do? If growing as a person is not the problem, what is? Problems arise when you hurt or damage other souls in the process of growing. When you harm other souls, refuse to honestly admit your mistakes, and continue to expand your ego even further, difficulties arise. What I want to say is that maybe your growth has become crooked when you are trying to grow straight. Are you sure you are not growing in a crooked way? Your desire to grow toward heaven is real and is the right thing to do. It is a natural feeling to have and you are allowed to have it. However, as you grow, are you sure your trunk and branches are not bending or jabbing others? You may believe you are aiming toward the sky, but you could actually be growing downward. I must point this out.

This is why we need self-reflection or the "principle of adjustment." You could live as freely as you wish if you were the only one living on earth. But the reality is that many people are allowed to live on earth and they, too, are given the freedom to grow as they like. God allows this situation because He knows the principle of adjustment will enable freedom to work properly. What this means is that we humans are allowed to grow freely without limit as long as we ensure that we live in harmony with others.

Some people may think of self-reflection as a negative or passive approach, or see it as too old and outdated, but that is not true at all. Self-reflection is like a stake that prevents a tree from bending; with it, a tree can grow straight. Because a tree grows toward the sky, it can grow limitlessly. But if its growth becomes crooked, it will eventually hit a wall or a house.

Therefore, self-reflection is not about blaming your shortcomings; rather, it is for your own benefit. By practicing self-reflection, you can prevent yourself from growing in a crooked way and from hurting or hindering others. But more importantly, it is the best way for you to grow limitlessly and this is the best way for you to be happy. You want to live freely because you want to be happy, right? That is why you want to do as you like, right? Self-reflection is a method that allows you to live that way. You will understand what I mean when you practice it. Those who have never practiced self-reflection tend to think of it as mere brakes that stop them from doing what they want, or as a restraint that confines them to a small room. They become afraid that, no matter what they do, they will fail or say the wrong words, and that no matter what they see, they will think of something negative. As a result, they feel bound and are unable to do anything. But this is just a delusion that people who are beginning to learn the Truth fall into. They fail to understand the essence of self-reflection because they are still new to the Truth. However, once they make a breakthrough, a truly wonderful world awaits them.

2
The First Step to Self-Reflection

The practice of self-reflection is the same as driving a car. I imagine many of you have a driver's license, or perhaps some of you have failed to get one. In any case, driving is very difficult in the beginning. You may wonder if you will ever learn how to drive such a "machine." All kinds of people are driving on the roads and I sometimes feel uneasy about it. Not everyone in this world has good reflexes; rather, many people probably have poor reflexes. Even so, everyone drives, including elderly people, housewives, and teenagers. I am often amazed to see that most people manage to stay safe every day. Not all drivers can play sports well, so why is it that they can drive? It is scary if you think about it. However, people gradually get used to driving. At first, it is difficult to handle the steering wheel, but it becomes easy once you get used to it.

It can be very nerve-racking to drive before you get used to it. Some people get so nervous that they sweat all over their bodies. I am actually speaking from my own experience. In the beginning, it is scary to drive a car, but it becomes easier once you get used to it; you can just hop in and drive off to a nearby station or store. The point is that you cannot drive smoothly when you think driving is difficult, but you will feel more comfortable once you have practiced enough.

Still, the process of driving a car seemed very complicated to me. I am the type of person who cannot be confident in something unless I learn it thoroughly. People like this study things deeply, so when they know very little, they feel very uneasy. To me, knowing only 10 to 20 percent of something is equal to knowing nothing. I still feel worried even if I know 50 percent. I wonder, "What is this? What is that?" and that makes me upset because I feel like I know nothing at all. I am sure there are people out there who feel like this.

Before you get used to driving a car, it feels difficult. The same can be said for self-reflection. Being told to self-reflect is like being told to get in a car and drive for the first time. Manual transmission cars stall easily unless you release the clutch pedal properly. People who usually drive cars with an automatic transmission cannot drive a manual car smoothly; they often make it stall and find it very difficult to drive. Self-reflection is very similar to that. Once you acquire the habit of reflecting on yourself, you will be able to do it as naturally as moving your arms and legs to change gears in a manual car.

Here is what I mean. You may think that self-reflection means secluding yourself in the mountains and meditating for a week. But as you make self-reflection a daily habit, you will be able to immediately reflect on your judgment regarding things you thought, spoke, and heard. You can do this automatically and gradually learn to control yourself. You need to develop the habit of noticing you are speaking badly about someone the moment the words come out instead of fretting over it for a year or two and then shedding tears of repentance. It is best to take back your words the moment you realize you have said something wrong. If you say right away, "I didn't mean it. I'm sorry," you will not need to apologize later or fret over it for a long time.

This is an extremely important practice. If you cause an accident, it is too late to then say "I should've driven a little more to the left"; you could be dead by then. You need to learn to naturally watch the flow of traffic and pedestrians while driving. When you think of self-reflection in this way, you will see that it is not so hard to do. You may think self-reflection restricts freedom and is difficult in the same way that driving is difficult because it requires learning how to steer while stepping on the brake and gas pedal. However, what if there were no traffic rules and people could drive as they liked? It would be chaotic. You would not know where a car would go or how fast it would move.

So what you think of as "freedom" is not really true freedom. Suppose people could drive on both the right and left lanes on the highway. That would not be "freedom."

Some may find it restricting to drive on only one side of the road, but it is because of these rules that people are allowed to drive freely. If people could drive any way they wanted, each person's movement would be more restricted; they would have to pay attention in all directions. If people were free to do anything, others would likely get in your way and limit your freedom. Just as there are traffic rules, there are "rules" and "skills and etiquette" involved in practicing self-reflection. It is said that both are important.

Let me now explain the skills for practicing self-reflection. It all comes down to controlling your mind. How can you control your mind? Not many people understand how to do this. You may be nodding, but 80 to 90 percent of people do not understand what I mean. You may say, "OK, I get it," but the truth is, you do not.

Can you control what you are going to think of next? Can you? I doubt it. I am sure you cannot. Various thoughts pop into your mind spontaneously, right? You may find all kinds of ideas forming in your mind like bubbles. They are like the bubbles that form in water when raindrops fall. You do not know where the raindrops will fall. Bubbles just form wherever the raindrops fall. That is how your mind works. Can you predict what you will be thinking in the next two or three minutes? Do you think you can control what you will be thinking? These questions may make you feel unsure of yourself. Most people have never thought about them. Many people do not have a habit of thinking deliberately. Surprisingly, many people, including each one of you, are not really thinking.

Can you stay still and just think about one particular thing? Can you focus your thoughts on just one thing? Perhaps your hands, eyes, or ears constantly need to be moving or doing something. I have seen many people like this. Some turn on the TV as soon as they enter the room. Are you one of these people? Once, when I went to my friend's house, I was surprised to see that he turned on the TV immediately after entering the room. He did so even though he had invited me to his house; that was his routine. He could not stand being in a quiet room without any stimulation, such as sounds, voices, or videos. There are actually many people like him. Some people need to turn on the stereo immediately after they get in their car.

Some people cannot stand even a minute of silence. They cannot help but do something, such as listening, watching, or speaking. I am sure there are many people like this among you. Please note that people like this cannot reflect on themselves. Unless they change their lifestyle, they will not be able to practice self-reflection. This is because they do not have a habit of deliberate thinking. They are always passive and are merely doing the task they are "trained" to do. They become restless unless something is constantly stimulating their brains. They are simply reacting to information such as sounds and colors that come in from the outside. They are reacting, rather than thinking deliberately. Deliberate thinking is different. It means to clearly visualize how you see things and what you think about them in an environment where all information is cut off. From this, you can see that thinking deliberately is not an easy practice. On hearing this, many people will realize, "Oh, I understand now. The reason I can't do self-reflection is probably because I can't stand not having the TV on." That is exactly right.

To practice self-reflection, you must be able to stay silent without saying anything, listening to anything, or seeing anything. It is important that you can bear being in this kind of environment. Unless you can do this, you will not be able to practice self-reflection. Can you be in a place where all information is shut out? You may get restless and feel like doing something. Just like how nicotine and alcohol addicts get withdrawals, you may grow impatient and agitated and look for something to do or read. But this is the critical point. While you are in an environment where all information is shut out, you need to become aware of your mind and realize, "There's something like a living creature in my chest. It has various thoughts and is emitting them. That's how it lives." So the first step of self-reflection is to shut out the outside world and look within. Because it is difficult to understand self-reflection intellectually, first, block out all outside information and set aside time to be alone.

When you are alone, you will be able to see the images of your thoughts and ideas for the first time. Your thoughts will be displayed on a black-and-white screen like a Charlie Chaplin movie. You will start to notice your thoughts and think, "This thought just crossed my mind," "I was thinking about him or her all day long," "I had this thought when I was eating lunch and that thought after I finished eating," or "Now, I'm thinking about what I thought about earlier. Surely, I'll think about something else a second later." By doing this, you will get into the habit of observing your thoughts. This is important.

Try to calm your mind for a while. Then, much like how muddy water that has been stirred up settles in many layers, your thoughts that have been agitated will also settle down. Many layers will be formed; the heavy ones will fall to the bottom, leaving the surface clear at the top. You will notice that some parts remain murky no matter how calm your mind gets. Heavy thoughts sink deeply, but there will still be something murky floating above them. You need to figure out what it is. What is causing the water to stay murky? You will then come to think, "I've heard about the

Eightfold Path. Maybe I can figure this out if I examine the unclear part based on this path." What is it that is making your mind stay murky and cloudy? You need to check it using the Eightfold Path.

3

Right View—Analyzing Cause and Effect

The first practice is Right View, or seeing rightly. This sounds vague and is not so easy to understand. But you can guess that it involves seeing with your eyes. So here is what you can do. Ask yourself what you saw today with your eyes and examine it. Let's say you met a particular person today. When you saw him or her, what did you think? Did you make the correct judgment about that person? The moment you saw the person, did you have any feeling of dislike toward him or her? What have you done through the act of "seeing"? Think about that.

The eye is a gateway through which information enters. What do you see with your eyes? This is an important checkpoint as you are always seeing other people through them. If you get used to practicing Right View, strangely enough, you will be able to see an image of yourself despite the fact that your eyes can only see the tip of your nose. Your eyes also capture an image of you. So if you reflect on how you have been today, you can visualize yourself from the time you woke up. Isn't that amazing? Although your eyes can only see the tip of your nose and your eyelashes, amazingly, you can picture yourself and how you have spent the day.

This shows that the eye is not merely a physical organ that captures light but is also a spiritual organ. Physically, your eyes are on your face, but spiritually, your eyes can see things in all directions, including yourself. Spiritually, they can see inward and outward. They can even go out of your body and see you from a distance. That is why you can visualize your own image or how you have been. Your spiritual eyes have this function.

If you further develop the function of your spiritual eyes, you will be able to see more things. You will not only be able to envision yourself and others but also see changes before and after an event. In other words, you will be able to see the cause and effect. When something happens, there is a result, meaning there is always a cause and an effect to everything.

Take, for example, your day today. Reflect on how you were before you came to this venue. Then, you may recall your day in the following way:

"The weather was not looking good. Then, it started raining. So I tried to hail a taxi to get to the venue, but I had a hard time catching one. When I finally got one, the taxi driver was in a bad mood, which made me upset, too. As a result, I was feeling grumpy even after getting to the venue and sitting in my seat." You may have thought so. "But then I listened to 'The Song of Holy Spirits' (recorded in the CD

'RYUHO OKAWA ALL TIME BEST I') and immediately got in a better mood."

You will find that you were thinking in this way. The cause and effect all make sense.

You should be able to analyze each scene in a course of events like this:

"Come to think of it, I felt much better after I listened to 'The Song of Holy Spirits,' but why was I feeling upset to begin with?" Then, upon reflecting on yourself, you will realize, "Oh, it was raining. What happened after that? I couldn't catch a taxi. After a while, I finally got one, but the driver was not very nice. So I thought, 'What's his license plate number? I'll call the taxi company later and file a complaint.' Then, I got off. That was why I came to this venue with a frown. And because I was grumpy, I didn't bother to say hello to someone I knew. They probably thought I was being rude."

If you reflect on yourself in this way, you will see the scenes in a course of events like a series of film frames. This analytical view is essential.

When practicing Right View in the Eightfold Path, it is important to understand the sequence of the causes and effects. "What was the cause of my action? What happened after that? The result must have caused something else to happen." You need to analyze yourself in this way.

Suppose you saw a man wearing a green outfit that gave you a bad impression of him. Why did you get a bad impression of him? By rewinding the film in your mind, you may find that someone who wore similar colored clothes had bad-mouthed you a year ago. You had forgotten about it, but since then, whenever you saw someone wearing green, you found them unpleasant. Your bad impression of the man was not due to his personality; his outfit just reminded you of the person who had bad-mouthed you. When you learn to analyze things in this way, you will be able to solve your problems easily.

People worry, suffer, complain, and fear because they do not understand why they think or feel a certain way. If they can understand why, most of their worries will disappear at that moment. Most people have no idea about the root cause of their problems. So it is important to figure out what that is. One of the ways to do this is to analyze what you see. This is Right View.

4
Right Speech—Examining Your Words

Earlier, I said that self-reflection is actually the principle of adjustment. In this sense, how you speak is extremely important. Words are crucial. If you reflect on yourself, you will likely come to see that in relationships, the words you use are the most important. The words you utter are the thing that will most often put you in a situation where you need to apologize to another person. This was not only taught by Shakyamuni Buddha but also by Jesus Christ. Jesus clearly taught, "Not what goes into the mouth defiles a man; but what comes out of the mouth, this defiles a man." He taught the importance of self-reflection on Right Speech. Indeed, words are important because they have spiritual power. Words play an extremely spiritual role in human activities on earth.

In this world, the vibrations of sound waves are translated into specific frequencies that are recognized as words through our eardrums. But in the Spirit World, spirits do not communicate with words transmitted through vibrations of air. Rather, their thoughts are transmitted directly to other spirits. Thoughts can certainly be translated into words, so if you want to know your thoughts, you need to check your speech. By examining your words, you will be able to understand clearly what your thoughts and ideas were. That is why it is essential to train yourself to examine your speech.

In a way, self-reflection on your speech is simple. In the previous section, I told you to reflect on your day as if you were watching a video of yourself. You can reflect on the past few years or your whole life in this way. The images you see at the time are like a four-panel or eight-panel comic strip without any speech bubbles. So you just need to fill in the bubbles with words. When you picture a scene in your mind, add your words and complete the "comic strip." What did you say at that moment? To practice self-reflection, you need to memorize and recall what you said.

Words that hurt others are mostly careless words. A person who speaks carelessly often does not remember saying hurtful things. So here is the best way to check your speech. When you say something, try to keep your eyes on the person you are speaking to. When you speak, the other person will receive your words within a second. Then, they will react in a certain way, either positive or negative. Their face may become bright or gloomy in reaction to your speech. You can check your speech by training yourself to observe the changes in the other person's facial expressions.

Those who hurt others with careless words tend to talk one-sidedly. The second they speak to someone, they look away. They say, "I don't like you," and look away. These people usually cannot look at the other person's face. So when you speak to someone, check if you are looking at the changes in his or her face. People who often use hurtful words do not look at the other person's face. To know whether you are using good words or bad words, see if you have the habit of observing the other person's face after you speak. If you do not have this habit, it is highly likely that you are making hurtful comments. You cannot look into another person's eyes when you say bad or hurtful things to them; this is human instinct. You will surely want to look away.

Therefore, when you speak, use words that enable you to keep observing the other person's facial expression and be attentive to them. In what instances can you keep looking at the other person's eyes or facial expressions? It must be when you say something that pleases them. When you tell someone, "You're beautiful," you want to see them smile, don't you? You will surely look at them. You would not look away after saying, "You're beautiful," or "What a great outfit." People will not cover their eyes when they say, "It's a beautiful day." When you anticipate that the other person will smile, you will want to see it. That is human nature.

I am talking about the yardstick for examining Right Speech. Reflecting on Right Speech at night after you get home is not enough. You can do it the moment you speak. Be a person who can keep looking at the eyes and expressions of the person you are speaking to. Of course, there are people who grin smugly at someone's strained, angry face. These people are eccentric and out of the norm. Some people take pleasure in upsetting others, but they must be aware that this is not normal. These people are an exception.

This is Right Speech. You can do it right away, and of course, at home before going to bed. Self-reflection before bed is also important, so to do that, you must practice remembering and reflecting on the words you spoke. If you say something bad to someone, it will show instantly, so the moment you notice your mistake, change your attitude immediately. Whether you meant it or not, if you notice that you have hurt the other person based on their expression, then make up for your mistake. Please compensate for it.

In tennis, if your first serve goes into the net, you get another chance. Similarly, if you make a slip of the tongue and hurt someone, add a few more words to correct your mistake right away. Tell them open-heartedly what you really meant. Perhaps you spoke that way simply because you were in a bad mood, sleep-deprived, hungover, or your muscles ached. These things will make it difficult to express the right words. Physical strains are hard to deal with, even for practitioners of the Truth. You can speak rightly when you have had enough sleep, have eaten well, and are full of energy, but it is difficult to do so when you are short on sleep or tired from overwork every day. There is only one way you can make amends if you say the wrong thing at such times, and that is to apologize. Explain to him or her, "I'm short on sleep," or "I'm not feeling well." That would be enough. It will surely heal his or her wound. You could say, "I'm sorry if I was rude. I've been a bit overworked." Then, the other person may understand. But if they do not understand why you said what you said, they will think it was their fault and suffer from it. So when you are out of sorts and say something wrong, honestly admit to it. If you are too embarrassed to apologize, just tell them you are out of sorts. Tell them, "I'm under the weather today." Whether or not you have this attitude will make a tremendous difference.

5

Right Thought—Examining Whether Your Thoughts Harm or Benefit Others

I have talked about Right View and Right Speech. I will now move on to the crucial part of the Eightfold Path, which is Right Thought. Whenever I talk about self-reflection, I can never really go into the details of Right Thought because it takes hours to explain it. Nevertheless, it is extremely important to practice Right Thought. In fact, we are undergoing life training to understand what Right Thought is.

Let me explain this in a way that is easier for you to visualize. Our mind is like a power generator that is constantly releasing energy; it is producing and discharging energy. Imagine a turbine and generator that is running in a hydroelectric power plant. Water falls from higher up to turn the turbine, which then generates electricity. Our minds work in a similar way because they are always generating something. This something is what you are releasing in the Spirit World. Each of you is like a generator releasing energy. The various facts and information you receive from the outside are like the falling water that turns the turbine.

With this, you are generating some kind of energy. Please understand the mind in this way.

Thus, what is emitted from your mind not only changes this world but also the other world. This is the truth. To put it simply, if you do not understand what the Real World in the afterlife is, imagine it as the world of the mind where only thoughts exist. There, you will not have arms, legs, a mouth, or a nose, but only thoughts. The Real World is made up of thoughts alone. Pure thoughts form heaven, while evil thoughts form hell. You, yourself, can make this distinction. Heaven and hell are not of the other world but are here in this world. They are an extension of this world. Just translate your thoughts and speech into an image or make them into a movie, and you should be able to tell if those thoughts and words are heavenly or hellish. If you cannot bear to watch the movie, then they are hellish. If it is pleasant to watch, then they are heavenly.

Your mind is constantly generating energy or projecting an image. Your mind, or thoughts emitted from your mind, are adding something to a new world. Thoughts are the "electric power" released from the generator, which is the mind. They can also be the "electrical phenomena" caused by electric power. This is the true nature of your thoughts.

You are an electric generator. So first, you must be determined to use this power for something meaningful.

Electric power itself is neutral in value. Originally, it was created to benefit us, but it can also be used for evil purposes. A single electric shock can kill a person. Electricity can power an electric stove or heater and warm things up, but if it is misused, it can cause a fire. Many things can happen. Moreover, high-voltage electricity can electrocute people. It is quite scary.

Speaking of electricity being misused, let me give an example from a movie. There is a James Bond film titled, *Licence to Kill*. In the movie, the new 007 sneaks into a dangerous enemy base. He fights the security guards in a room with many fish tanks, one of which houses an electric eel. The guard has a gun, but James Bond is unarmed. So Bond grabs a long hook nearby and yanks the guard from underneath. The guard falls into the tank and is electrocuted by the eel. My point here is that electricity is not always used for a good purpose. It can be used for a bad purpose too, such as killing someone.

So, what you think and the thoughts you have in your mind work like electricity; they discharge energy. This energy can paralyze others or it can be used efficiently and be a benefit for society, like the way electricity powers electrical appliances. It can be dangerous, but there is also a positive side to it. To produce a positive effect, you must deliver it properly, much like how electricity is delivered to houses with a suitable voltage by using power lines. The same is true with your thoughts. You can generate thoughts in any way you like; for example, you can think of abusing others or apologizing to them on your knees. But you must use your thoughts well and make them beneficial. You must not generate them and just let them flow out freely in an uncontrolled manner.

When you realize that your thoughts are actually affecting the world, you will become aware of how big a duty you have. Controlling your thoughts is a serious duty. The fact that hell is expanding means many people are emitting negative thoughts. A lot of energy is being used for the wrong purposes, so we must use it for good purposes instead.

Then what is a good purpose? How should we use our "energy"? Here is the correct way to use it: Use your thoughts to make many people happier. This is the key point. The yardstick for checking Right Thought is to ask yourself whether your thoughts were used to expand happiness or block happiness. Right Thought can be summarized into this single point.

There are many other methods of self-reflection in the Eightfold Path, but I especially want to emphasize the importance of Right Thought. Thoughts are the energy that creates the world. They can either harm or benefit others. They can make the world either happier or unhappier. In a nutshell, to check Right Thought, see if your thoughts or the energies you are emitting are beneficial to others. Reflect deeply on whether they are improving yourself, who are a part of God, and the world. Set aside time to be silent and reflect on each of your thoughts. Did they truly help improve the world created by God? Are they contributing in that direction? Please analyze this carefully. That is all. Thank you very much.

CHAPTER FIVE

What Is Unlimited Love?

The Eighth Public Lecture of 1989

Originally recorded in Japanese on November 12, 1989
at Tokyo Bay NK Hall in Chiba Prefecture, Japan
and later translated into English.

1
Love Is the Power to Unite One Another

Today, my lecture is titled, "What Is Unlimited Love?" This is probably the first time many of you have come to one of my lectures, so let me start by talking about a familiar topic.

A few days ago, in Eastern Europe, the wall that had been encircling West Berlin was brought down. It was a historic event and, like many others, I watched the news on TV. There were family members and friends who, although they were German and lived in the same city, had not been able to see each other for many decades. This was simply because some of them lived in East Berlin and others lived in West Berlin. This situation lasted for a long time. I saw many people from the East climbing over the wall and streaming into the West, and many people from the West gathering to welcome them. Looking at their faces, I could see the meaning of love.

Love is the power to unite one another. However, we unknowingly build huge "walls" between ourselves and others based on the ideas, beliefs, ideologies, and prejudices we have acquired since birth. Ever since I awakened to the Truth, I have met many people and listened to their worries and problems. From the perspective of love, I found there is only one issue. That is, there is a wall, a border, a boundary, a barrier, or a fence between them and others. Love is a power that unites people. On the other hand, the power that opposes love is a power that rejects others and severs ties between people. It is also a power that makes people who get along hate each other.

If you look at the world objectively, you will find these two opposing powers fighting each other. Someone who loved another person yesterday may suddenly find fault with them today and be pointing it out. They may wonder how they could have possibly gotten along with the person and fall under the illusion that they had not been their true selves until now. Inner conflicts like these occur again and again in the course of our lives as we live as human beings. Yes, that's right. As we meet various types of people and live together in a community, we constantly find ourselves in between these two opposing powers. Will you choose the power that unites people or give in to the power that rejects them? Simply put, we are constantly supplying energy to one of the two.

Now, today I am not simply saying, "Christianity and other religions teach that love is a wonderful thing, so please abide by the teachings of love." I want you to consider the issue of love from the perspective of your daily life. I do not intend to force a particular dogma or set of values on you. Each person has a unique and wonderful nature or a good tendency of the mind. I have faith in this wonderful tendency in each person's mind. So I will talk about love today, not because of its wonderful qualities, but because I believe that each of you has this wonderful part in your mind. I want to appeal to that wonderful part in you. So, today's lecture will have to do with the essence of human beings.

2
The Other World Undeniably Exists

The 6,000 of you have gathered here today through some kind of connection. Almost all of you must have come across these ideas we call the "Truth" at some point in your lives. Or perhaps some of you may have come here simply because your friends invited you.

However, nowadays in Japan, even the term *God* seems to have become obsolete. A lot of people may be embarrassed to even mention the word. Many of you probably believe in God, but may not be able to talk about it to others. But how can you believe, learn, and teach others about God's Truth if you are hesitant to even talk about it? It may seem extremely difficult for you to do so.

Looking back at my own experiences, I am fully aware of just how difficult it is to get people to understand the Truth. Even if you have understood it and are convinced of it to some extent, I know how hard it is to convey your beliefs to others. Nevertheless, I dare say to you: The fact is fact, the truth is truth.

If the Truth we teach was completely fake and was only something we pursued out of curiosity or to deceive a lot of people, then the last eight years I have spent exploring the

Truth would have been in vain. However, as someone who has had firsthand experience of the Spirit World, I must tell you the following, no matter what the cost.

On March 23, 1981, I received a revelation from a world that cannot be seen with our eyes. Ever since I was born, I did not react so badly to words like *God* or *spirits*. I certainly believed in the existence of God, spirits, and the afterworld, but I had only classified these ideas in my head as just a possibility. However, after I received a revelation from the heavenly part of the world eight years ago, I could no longer say that I only believed in the afterworld 50, 60, 80, or 99 percent—it was 100 percent real. Its existence was undeniable. There was no room for doubt.

Even if 50, 60, or 70 percent of Japanese people today laugh at this idea, the fact is fact and the truth is truth. As someone who trusts his conscience and who believes that trusting his good conscience is the only way to the Truth, I cannot tell a lie. The fact is fact, the truth is truth. The spiritual phenomena I experienced were not a one-time event; they were not something that only happened on that day. For the last eight years, not a single day has passed without me receiving a spiritual revelation.

Now, I have a physical body and call myself Ryuho Okawa, but the one speaking to you is me and also not me. As I speak, I am receiving guidance and inspiration from high spirits in a world far beyond this one. I am aware of this fact 100 percent. That is why I am addressing you directly in this venue while looking at your faces.

As proof of this fact, I have already published over 80 books, one after another (as of the lecture). This year alone, I have published 30 books. This would not have been possible if they were mere fabrications. If it were not for the revelations from the invisible world, it would have been impossible for me to write as many books. In this way, I have continuously presented you with the Truth in the form of writing.

But alas! Despite having a culture of high literacy, so many people in Japan have yet to awaken to the Truth. So many people continue to live with a mistaken view of life. No matter how many books I publish, it is hard to get them to everyone.

Selling three to four million copies of my books is far from enough. I want to sell at least 120 million copies, of course. I want everyone to read at least one book of Truth. That is the minimum requirement. That is because over 100 million people who live in Japan do not know about the true world. They believe that denying the invisible world makes them intellectual.

3
Fighting against Disbelief

What is worse, this is not only true for people in general but also for people in religious circles, such as Buddhist monks and Christian priests. These religious professionals also strictly deny the facts that I convey.

So here is what I want to ask Christians: Do you believe that miracles only occurred 2,000 years ago? Do you believe that God only existed 2,000 years ago? Did God only come down to earth in those times? Did spirits only exist in those times? Do you believe that God has kept silent since then and continues to stay silent to this day? Do you think that Jesus, in whom you believe, has been dormant ever since he was crucified on Golgotha? Do you believe such absurdities? This is what I want to ask you.

In the same way, here is what I want to ask Buddhists: Look at what you are doing. Did Shakyamuni Buddha teach about funeral procedures and manners? Did Buddha encourage you to recite the sutra in classical Chinese? Did Buddha teach such things? This is what I want to ask you.

What Buddha wanted to teach is written precisely in my book, *The Rebirth of Buddha*. Buddha taught all people, including monks and nuns, about real life and the view of the world that real human beings should have. He did not teach funeral procedures and he did not tell monks to wear special robes, light incense, or kneel before a gravestone. He taught the way humans should live. He taught that the essence of humans is exactly the same as God or Buddha.

Humans are great because they have the very nature of God or Buddha within them. But ever since they were born on earth, they have been blinded by worldly delusions, desires, and attachments. As a result, they have long forgotten the right way to live. No matter how polished a mirror may be, if it is covered in dirt or dust, it will not reflect the correct image. Likewise, even though we are children of God or children of Buddha, we must always explore Right Mind and strive to eliminate the mistakes in our minds one by one. Otherwise, the mirror of our minds will not reflect this world or other people correctly; instead, it will reflect a distorted image. Why do you remain complacent about living in such a distorted world? Why do you think it is right? Why do you accept it as it is? Why don't you feel sad about it? Why don't you question it?

The Bible describes how Jesus struggled and suffered to spread the Truth during the three years of his missionary work. By reading it, we can see that Jesus' greatest challenge was the fight against people's disbelief. His battle for the Truth, which he fought from the age of 30 to 33, was a fight against disbelief. His fight boiled down to this single point. It is unbelievable how many people back then did not believe in Jesus' words. One after another, people spoke out doubting his words, the miracles he performed, and the truth he taught. These stories in the Bible are too sad for me to read.

Why are people so full of distrust when they are all children of God? Why do they assume that people always lie? Why do they assume that what they cannot see with their eyes does not exist? Why do they assume that what they cannot hear with their ears is not real? Why do they assume that what they cannot understand with their brains is mere fiction? Humans cannot even measure the height of a mountain using their own height. So how can they possibly understand God's Will with their limited understanding? How can they truly grasp the vastness of the universe with their limited perception?

At the core of disbelief lies the boundless arrogance of human beings. It would be good if you could truly understand that you are a child of God and value yourself accordingly. But the problem is that people believe in something completely different. They think that they can judge society, the world, and others as if they were God. These kinds of arrogant people existed 2,000 years ago, 2,500 years ago, and they even exist today. I believe that teaching about love on earth is also a fight against disbelief. Selfish people cannot believe that there are selfless people who give love to others without expecting any reward or without selfish motives. People have regressed this far. They think that this world is based entirely on "give and take." Still, a "give and take" attitude is better than "take and take." Oh, how many people there are who think of just taking love from others.

Both Christianity and Buddhism teach that desires and attachments are not good. But desires are not actually evil in and of themselves. The essence of a desire is a wish to grow, which is a tendency everyone has. Unfortunately, however, this tendency has turned into a selfish desire for some people; they want to achieve success for themselves, even if it comes at a cost to others. God, or Buddha, has never taught such a thing. How did people come to live with a narrow, selfish love? Why have people become so pathetic? You have to ask these questions. When someone is kind to you, do you assume that they have a selfish motivation or do you believe it is their natural disposition? We must be determined to get rid of doubtful tendencies like this.

4

Knowing the Great Love of God

Some of you may think of faith as an outdated, worn-out, and ridiculous idea. Perhaps you have heard others say this. Each person has their own ideas about the word *faith*. But, I would like to define faith in a new light.

Faith is based on the truth that we are able to live thanks to the great powers we receive from the invisible world. To be more specific, these powers are the powers of your guardian spirit or the powers of guiding spirits who are on a higher level. They are also the powers of even higher divine spirits, as well as the powers of even greater beings that do not possess human characteristics. I have seen their powers with my own eyes. I have heard their voices with my own ears. And I have spoken their words through my own mouth. Because I have been talking with them every day for more than eight years, there is no room for me to deny their existence. It is an undeniable fact that another world exists beyond this one. Its inhabitants are invisible and without a physical body, but they have the same nature as the purest part of your mind. They represent the most refined part of you.

When you remove the errors or dirt from your mind, a pure and innocent mind that wants to love many people will appear. Spiritual beings in the heavenly world all have pure minds like this, and they exist in great numbers. They are people who lived on earth before you. They left this world tens, hundreds, or thousands of years ago. There is a world for those who lived a wonderful life and graduated from this world. These beings are not living for themselves. Although you cannot see them or notice them, they are always watching over you. Day and night, they watch over you as you live in this third dimensional Phenomenal World—a world that looks like a miniature garden to them. They never stop thinking about you.

People who have gained a shallow level of spiritual knowledge may arrogantly argue, "If such handy guardian spirits exist, why has my life been so full of misery? Why has it been full of pain and suffering? It doesn't make any sense. I hear they have great power like the Almighty God, but if they do, why didn't they come and help me when I was in agony? Why didn't they help me open up a path when I was failing?" People with only a superficial understanding of spirituality may say things like this.

However, I say unto you: Your guardian spirit feels happy when you are happy and sad when you are sad. In the invisible world, there are beings who share your sadness as their own. They cannot bear to leave you in sadness and they secretly weep in a world that you cannot perceive.

There are beings like that. Their love is shed limitlessly onto each one of you, just like how the sun shines upon us all. It is shed equally on the good-hearted and the wicked, just like blessed rain.

In the course of your life, you sometimes live in ways that please God and at other times in ways that do not please God. Sometimes, you may feel like you have been rewarded and at other times, you may feel like you have been punished severely. Even so, regardless of what you do or think, God watches over you, just like parents watch over their young children. There is a Being that forgives you completely and is shedding tears for you. Believing in this Being is faith.

Faith is not dubious. It is definitely not a means for you to gain worldly benefits. Faith is to know the true nature of the world we live in and to understand the essence of human beings. This is what people have called "faith." People today are fascinated by science, so they may find it difficult to accept the concept of faith. Therefore, I will call it "science" instead. In order to call it "science," I have continuously published many books and given many lectures for people to study. I do so because I want you to know the Truth. I want you to confirm it with your own eyes and your own ears. If possible, I want you to grasp it with your own heart and soul.

I just said that faith means to know the true world. So what does it mean to know the true world? It means to know the great love that surrounds us. No one can live out their life all by themselves. This is true from the perspective of this world and the world beyond this one. Can any of you claim to have lived all on your own? Even if you just consider your life in this world, how many people have supported you behind the scenes?

This applies to me as much as it does to you. There are people who designed and built this venue and people who are running it. There are people who made this mic as well as people who made my suit and tie. There are also those who made the fabric used to make my suit and tie. The same is true for cars and other things. We cannot accomplish anything on our own. This is the reality of modern human society. How can you remain unaware of this?

We cannot see all the work that is done by people who are alive. Even though we cannot see it all, we still benefit from it. Everything you need to live in this world has been given to you. Many people are sustaining your life unknowingly, despite having no personal connection with you. What is more, in the world beyond this one, many more beings are living with the hope of helping you.

Some misguided religious leaders urge people to hold ancestral memorial services and say that the souls of their ancestors are still lost and need to be saved. They try to create new believers in this way. I do not deny that this is a possibility, but a person who has lived a decent life in this world will definitely remain decent in the other world. People who are respectable in this world will continue to be respectable in the other world. Why would great people appear before you as bloody ghosts? How can you accept this kind of view of the Spirit World? I certainly cannot. Why would people who worked hard for many others and lived with a pure heart turn into such pitiful beings? That could never happen.

Those who lived with love for many people in this world will surely continue to live with love in the other world. They will surely live to help others. They will surely try to help those who come after them. Are there any parents who hate their children? Are there any grandparents who hate their grandchildren? No, of course not. Can you imagine how earnestly those who have left this world before you are praying and wishing for your happiness day in and day out? Despite that, people ignore their wishes and continue to say, "There's no such thing as the other world, spirits, or God. It's nonsense." Who will take responsibility for the sin of having this mistaken belief? It is none other than those who keep on believing in it.

5
All That Matters Is Your Mind

Heaven and hell really do exist. I have seen them with my own eyes. Even now, I can see into both of them. I sometimes talk with the spirits in heaven and sometimes with those in hell. Heaven and hell truly exist. This is 100 percent true. There is no room for doubt. And it is each person's mind that leads them to either heaven or hell. It is your own mind that determines where you end up; it is not up to other people.

People tend to think of their happiness as the fruit of their own hard work and blame others or the environment for their unhappiness. However, the afterworld I have seen does not allow excuses. No matter what environment you are in or who you are surrounded by, what matters is how you live in the circumstances given to you. Everything depends on your mind. In the afterworld, you will be asked, "We understand your life was hard. We admit you lived through your life in a tough environment. But what mindset did you have while living a tough life? How did you view your hardship? Did you see it negatively or positively? Did you just blame others?"

Heaven and hell do not only exist in the invisible world; they also exist within you, right now. Looking into your mind, many of you probably think that you are unhappy. That may be why you have come to my lecture to find some clues about how to be happy. But I dare say to you that it is your own mind that is making you unhappy. It is also your own mind that will make you happy. Those who have learned the mystical nature of the mind and succeeded in finding happiness in any circumstance will go to heaven.

Heaven is not a world for esoteric people. The people you find who are wonderful, pure in heart, and who you want to associate with will go there without exception. It is a normal world. To return to such a normal world is easy. Despite that, many people today are unable to achieve this simple thing. In the modern age, more than half of the people on earth fail to return to heaven. Spiritually, this means that over 50 percent of people are suffering from some kind of mental illness. How can you be proud of this modern civilization when you cannot even control your own mind? How can you say you have become advanced? How much have you advanced compared to those who lived 2,000, 3,000, or 10,000 years ago? Have you truly improved and become wonderful?

Since ancient times, those who have been called "greats" or "saints" have continuously taught one truth: Your mind is all that matters. It is your real entity. Whether you are happy or unhappy in life depends on how you control your mind.

They have taught this single truth over and over for tens of thousands of years.

I have been telling you to control your mind, but many of you may have suddenly lost confidence in yourself and are finding it difficult to practice. However, let me repeat the following. There are many beings who support and encourage you in the world beyond this one. You must know this. They are calling out and shouting, "Come this way. You'll fail with thoughts like that. Think and live in this way instead." You are getting a lot of support and encouragement, so why don't you listen? Are you telling me that you cannot hear their voices? Then let me tell you. You can actually hear them.

How can you do that? Just clear your mind. Reflect on the mistakes you have made. Look back at the several decades of your life, and if you find that you have held mistaken thoughts, correct them. If you have done something wrong, sincerely apologize to those who suffered as a result of your actions, ask God for forgiveness, and pledge not to make the same mistake again.

By doing this, your mind will be purified. When that happens, tears will flow. As you look back on your past, you will not be able to hold back your tears, and this proves that you are a child of God. You shed tears because you cannot remain indifferent to your wrong deeds. That is how you were created to be. You were designed to live rightly. That is why tears will not stop welling up from the depths of your heart even though you were not taught to shed tears in this way.

If you are living with wrong thoughts or actions, please make sure you experience moments like this. When you do, you will feel something warm embracing you. At times, you will receive clear guidance. At other times, you will notice that the obstacle blocking your way was removed and that a new life is unfolding powerfully like a torrent of water. One door may close and another may open. You will experience these things. When you refine and purify your mind and are grateful for the support you are being given from the invisible world, you will find that many kinds of phenomena like this occur.

Although I might sound like I am more respectable than all of you, I, too, have experienced this. I looked back on how I had lived wrongly. I reflected thoroughly on how I had been living with wrong thoughts and with a false self that was full of vanity and pride. I thought, "If I continue to live this way, I'll end up ruined and fall to the depths of hell. I've lived in vanity and self-deception without gratitude. I've lived selfishly. There's no way I'll be forgiven. I must change myself now. I must start over from scratch. I have been bound by desire, fame, and various things that have benefited me, but I must free my mind from them. I must abandon all of these thoughts and stand empty-handed. With nothing in my hands and with a clear mind, I will start from scratch. I will reset my life and start over from zero." When I became determined like this, the phenomenon that I predicted would occur to you occurred to me. The spirits who had been guarding and guiding me started talking to me. What I experienced was surprisingly a simple and natural phenomenon. This is what humans should naturally experience. But alas, so many people fail to do what they can do naturally. This happens because they do not learn about it anywhere. It is also because there is no end to the number of people who mock these true teachings.

As humans acquire knowledge and become a little intelligent, they soon start to show disdain for others, see them as childish, and criticize their ways of thinking and living. But think about it. Who do you think pleases God more, someone with a pure heart or someone with knowledge from tens of thousands of books crammed into their brain? The answer is clear. God is pleased with someone who humbly accepts the truth as the truth and strives to live by it; that is how humans should be. Why is it so difficult for humans to return to how they were intended to be? It is because you have accumulated so much wrong knowledge and distorted your value judgments with wrong will.

Examine your value judgments. You are probably influenced by other people's values. I am sure you cannot escape temptation when people tell you, "You can earn the respect of others if you work for this company" or "You'll be regarded highly if you attend this school." This world is filled with all kinds of temptations, and our minds are tainted by earthly values like this every single day. We must firmly resist them. Unless we regain our true minds, there will be no meaning to our lives at all.

Without a strong foundation, whatever you build on top of it will just collapse. This is called a "castle built on sand." Nothing can be built on sand. Having the right view of life as your basis is vital. If you have this, you can truly be successful and respected by others. Your self-realization or fame will also be genuine. It is wonderful when people who have the right view of life and who know about the true world succeed and develop themselves out of love for many people. Make no mistake about this starting point. It is fine for you to study and collect a lot of knowledge. But if your basic view of life is wrong, what you study will be completely useless.

This may sound harsh. But, to be blunt, unless you pass through this first gate, you will never be happy. Even if you manage to fulfill your desires using various theories for worldly success, you will never know what kind of world awaits you after death.

I have repeatedly said that you can only bring your mind with you when you leave this world—only your mind. You cannot bring your fortune or your social status. If your mind is the only thing you can bring back with you, what could be more important than to refine it? That is the only way to be happy. It is that simple. Starting today, how much brighter, purer, and full of love for many people can you fill your mind with? This is the way to triumph in life every day.

6
What Is Unlimited Love?

I often ponder the theme of freedom, which is only granted to humans. The issue of East and West Germany that I spoke about in the beginning is also an issue of choosing between freedom and control. The West is free, whereas the East is controlled. From the perspective of the East, the free world is full of corruption and decadence, so they try to prevent this from happening by controlling their people. From the perspective of the free world, a controlled society makes people suffer because it does not allow individuals to express themselves or realize their goals. Both sides are trying to guide people in a better direction, but they contradict each other.

Watching people go over the Berlin Wall, I could see very well why God granted freedom to humans. It is because freedom is the greatest happiness. However, it is meaningless if people only create confusion and destruction or hurt others as a result of having freedom. That is why God teaches humans, "I'll grant you freedom, but with freedom comes responsibility. This means that you are responsible for controlling your own mind. Becoming happy is not your right, but your duty. Everyone has a duty to become happy by controlling their own mind."

This is the price of freedom. The price of freedom is the duty to become happy by controlling your mind. What is most important in controlling your mind? It is to repent and correct your thoughts and deeds. If you have wrong thoughts, correct them right away and think good thoughts. If you did something wrong, pledge to never make the same mistake again, apologize to the people you troubled, and ask for God's forgiveness. Then, strive to build a wonderful life from that day on.

God gives humans the greatest freedom, and at the same time, allows humans to practice self-reflection to correct the mistakes they have made as a result of exercising their freedom. God allows people to enjoy happiness in this way. I believe this is the unlimited love that God has given us. Everyone is given freedom and the chance to self-reflect when they make mistakes. Through self-reflection, we can fulfill our duty to be happy. If this is not unlimited love, what is?

Each of us must realize how magnificent and precious this love of God is. I pray that my lecture today will help you realize this. Thank you very much.

Afterword

When I read the manuscript of this book, I was overjoyed. I was deeply impressed by how I was giving my all back then, as well. Content-wise, Happy Science had already been showing signs of being the number one religious group in Japan two years before it was actually certified as a religious corporation.

Even though my ideas about a political system slightly changed after I founded our political party, the Happiness Realization Party, in 2009, you can still get a good understanding of my basic ways of thinking through this book.

It feels as though it was only yesterday that I taught the Eightfold Path in a simple way in Kagawa Prefecture, as I felt that the audience would find it too difficult to understand. It wasn't until years later that I taught it in much more detail.

Around the time I gave the lecture, "What Is Unlimited Love?" I witnessed the historic moment when the Berlin Wall fell and the people of East and West Germany united as one. I wonder if younger people nowadays can understand what was going on at the time of this lecture.

This book is very much the history of my own path to enlightenment in times of historical moments.

Ryuho Okawa
Master & CEO of Happy Science Group
February 21, 2021

For a deeper understanding of
The Way to Human Perfection
see other books below by Ryuho Okawa:

The Laws of the Sun [New York, IRH Press, 2018]
Rojin, Buddha's Mystical Power [New York, IRH Press, 2021]
Invincible Thinking [New York, IRH Press, 2017]
The Rebirth of Buddha [New York, IRH Press, 2022]

ABOUT THE AUTHOR

Founder and CEO of Happy Science Group.

Ryuho Okawa was born on July 7th 1956, in Tokushima, Japan. After graduating from the University of Tokyo with a law degree, he joined a Tokyo-based trading house. While working at its New York headquarters, he studied international finance at the Graduate Center of the City University of New York. In 1981, he attained Great Enlightenment and became aware that he is El Cantare with a mission to bring salvation to all humankind.

In 1986, he established Happy Science. It now has members in 171 countries across the world, with more than 700 branches and temples as well as 10,000 missionary houses around the world.

He has given over 3,500 lectures (of which more than 150 are in English) and published over 3,200 books (of which more than 600 are Spiritual Interview Series), and many are translated into 42 languages. Along with *The Laws of the Sun* and *The Laws of Hell*, many of the books have become best sellers or million sellers. To date, Happy Science has produced 27 movies under his supervision. He has given the original story and concept and is also the Executive Producer. He has also composed music and written lyrics of over 450 pieces.

Moreover, he is the Founder of Happy Science University and Happy Science Academy (Junior and Senior High School), Founder and President of the Happiness Realization Party, Founder and Honorary Headmaster of Happy Science Institute of Government and Management, Founder of IRH Press Co., Ltd., and the Chairperson of NEW STAR PRODUCTION Co., Ltd. and ARI Production Co., Ltd.

BOOKS BY RYUHO OKAWA

Basic Teachings of Happy Science

The Ten Principles from El Cantare Volume I

Ryuho Okawa's First Lectures
on His Basic Teachings

Paperback • 232 pages • $16.95
ISBN: 978-1-942125-85-3 (Dec. 15, 2021)

This book contains the historic lectures given on the first five principles of the Ten Principles of Happy Science by the author, Ryuho Okawa, who is revered as the World Teacher. These lectures produced an enthusiastic fellowship in Happy Science Japan and became the foundation of the current global utopian movement. You can learn the essence of Okawa's teachings and the secret behind the rapid growth of the Happy Science movement in simple language.

The Ten Principles from El Cantare Volume II

Ryuho Okawa's First Lectures
on His Wish to Save the World

Paperback • 272 pages • $16.95
ISBN: 978-1-942125-86-0 (May 3, 2022)

A sequel to *The Ten Principles from El Cantare Volume I.* Volume II reveals the Creator's three major inventions; the secret of the creation of human souls, the meaning of time, and 'happiness' as life's purpose. By reading this book, you can not only improve yourself but learn how to make differences in society and create an ideal, utopian world.

What Is Happy Science?

Best Selection of Ryuho Okawa's Early Lectures (Volume 1)

Paperback • 256 pages • $17.95
ISBN: 978-1-942125-99-0 (Aug. 25, 2023)

The Best Selection series is a collection of Ryuho Okawa's passionate lectures during the ages of 32 to 33 that revealed the mission and goal of Happy Science. This book contains the eternal Truth, including the meaning of life, the secret of the mind, the true meaning of love, the mystery of the universe, and how to end hatred and world conflicts.

The Laws of Happiness

Love, Wisdom, Self-Reflection and Progress

Paperback • 264 pages • $16.95
ISBN: 978-1-942125-70-9 (Aug. 28, 2020)

Happiness is not found outside us; it is found within us. It is in how we think, how we look at our lives, and how we devote our hearts to the work we do. Discover how the Fourfold Path of Love, Wisdom, Self-Reflection and Progress create a life of sustainable happiness.

Developmental Stages of Love - The Original Theory

Philosophy of Love in My Youth

Hardcover • 200 pages • $17.95
ISBN: 978-1-942125-94-5 (Jun. 15, 2022)

This book is about author Ryuho Okawa's original philosophy of love which serves as the foundation of love in the chapter three of *The Laws of the Sun*. It consists of series of short essays authored during his ages of 25 to 28 while he was working as a young promising business elite at an international trading company after attaining the Great Enlightenment in 1981. This is an excellent book to contemplate the true meaning of love in our everyday life.

El Cantare Trilogy

The first three volumes of the Laws Series, *The Laws of the Sun*, *The Golden Laws*, and *The Laws of Eternity* make a trilogy that completes the basic framework of the teachings of God's Truths. *The Laws of the Sun* discusses the structure of God's Laws, *The Golden Laws* expounds on the doctrine of time, and *The Laws of Eternity* reveals the nature of space.

The Laws of the Sun

One Source, One Planet, One People

Paperback • 288 pages • $15.95
ISBN: 978-1-942125-43-3 (Oct. 15, 2018)

IMAGINE IF YOU COULD ASK GOD why He created this world and what spiritual laws He used to shape us–and everything around us. If we could understand His designs and intentions, we could discover what our goals in life should be and whether our actions move us closer to those goals or farther away.

At a young age, a spiritual calling prompted Ryuho Okawa to outline what he innately understood to be universal truths for all humankind. In *The Laws of the Sun*, Okawa outlines these laws of the universe and provides a road map for living one's life with greater purpose and meaning. In this powerful book, Ryuho Okawa reveals the transcendent nature of consciousness and the secrets of the multidimensional universe as well as the meaning of humans that exist within it. By understanding the different stages of love and following the Buddhist Eightfold Path, he believes we can speed up our eternal process of development. *The Laws of the Sun* shows the way to realize true happiness–a happiness that continues from this world through the other.

The Golden Laws

History through the Eyes of
the Eternal Buddha

E-book • 204 pages • $13.99
ISBN: 978-1-941779-82-8 (Sep. 24, 2015)

Throughout history, Great Guiding Spirits have been present on Earth in both the East and the West at crucial points in human history to further our spiritual development. *The Golden Laws* reveals how Divine Plan has been unfolding on Earth, and outlines 5,000 years of the secret history of humankind. Once we understand the true course of history, through past, present and into the future, we cannot help but become aware of the significance of our spiritual mission in the present age.

The Laws of Eternity

El Cantare Unveils the Structure of
the Spirit World

Paperback • 200 pages • $17.95
ISBN: 978-1-958655-16-0 (May 15, 2024)

"Where do we come from and where do we go after death?" This unparalleled book offers us complete answers to life's most important questions that we all are confronted with at some point or another.

This book reveals the eternal mysteries and the ultimate secrets of Earth's Spirit Group that have been covered by the veil of legends and myths. Encountering the long-hidden Eternal Truths that are revealed for the first time in human history will change the way you live your life now.

New Books

The Eternal Buddha

Now, Here, Is the Imperishable Light

Hardcover • 180 pages • $17.95
ISBN: 978-1-958655-19-1 (Sep 15, 2024)

This book is a powerful source of guidance for those seeking Truth.

Embedded within, you will find the infinite wisdom of Eternal Buddha and come to realize that you are not just a physical being, but an eternal soul of brilliant light.

This book will help you discover the true origin of your soul, why you have chosen to be born in this time, and why having faith is important.

Through the words of Eternal Buddha, unlock the boundless treasures of enlightenment given to humankind in this modern era.

The Earth says, "All you need is Love"

Overcoming the trials of humanity with God's guidance

Paperback • 152 pages • $20.00
ISBN: 979-8-88737-119-1 (August, 2024)

In this book, Ryuho Okawa warns against the harsh trials that are to hit humanity and describes what we should know and do now. To overcome the many conflicts that are happening around the world, what humanity needs is the power of love that is based on faith. This is the key to bringing peace on Earth.

Faithful to the Truth

Realizing God's Vision of Future Society

Paperback • 164 pages • $20.00
ISBN: 979-8-887371-12-2 (Apr. 24, 2024)

The spiritual truth and the forecasts written in this book are messages from God that people worldwide should know right now. The world is on the verge of collapse. So, now is the time when people should listen to what Okawa is saying, as he is the one who knows the Truth, who can see God's vision, and who is trying to guide humanity in the right direction.

The Miracle Power to Overcome Illness

Healing Through Faith

Paperback • 256 pages • $17.95
ISBN: 978-1-958655-17-7 (Jul 15, 2024)

With his deep spiritual insight, Okawa points out the spiritual causes of mental and physical problems and the ways to overcome them. Transcend your worldly understanding of illness, awaken to the power of faith, and make efforts to improve yourself, step by step. Then, surely, you will receive the miracle power from the heavenly world.

Bestselling Buddhist Titles

The Essence of Buddha

The Path to Enlightenment

Paperback • 208 pages • $14.95
ISBN: 978-1-942125-06-8 (Oct.1, 2016)

In this book, Ryuho Okawa imparts in simple and accessible language his wisdom about the essence of Shakyamuni Buddha's philosophy of life and enlightenment—teachings that have been inspiring people all over the world for over 2,500 years. By offering a new perspective on core Buddhist thoughts that have long been cloaked in mystique, Okawa brings these teachings to life for modern people. *The Essence of Buddha* distills a way of life that anyone can practice to achieve a life of self-growth, compassionate living, and true happiness.

The True Eightfold Path

Guideposts for Self-Innovation

Paperback • 256 pages • $16.95
ISBN: 978-1-942125-80-8 (Mar. 30, 2021)

This book explains how we can apply the Eightfold Path, one of the main pillars of Shakyamuni Buddha's teachings, as everyday guideposts in the modern age to achieve self-innovation to live better and make positive changes in these uncertain times.

The Rebirth of Buddha

My Eternal Disciples, Hear My Words

Paperback • 280 pages • $17.95
ISBN: 978-1-942125-95-2 (Jul. 15, 2022)

These are the messages of Buddha who has returned to this modern age as promised to His eternal beloved disciples, in simple words and poetic style. Once you start reading these passages, your soul will be replenished and you will remember why you chose this era to be born into with Buddha. Listen to the voices of your Eternal Master and awaken to your calling.

Rojin, Buddha's Mystical Power

Its Ultimate Attainment in Today's World

Paperback • 224 pages • $16.95
ISBN: 978-1-942125-82-2 (Sep. 24, 2021)

In this book, Ryuho Okawa has redefined the traditional Buddhist term *Rojin* to fit modern society as follows: The ability for individuals with great spiritual powers to live in the world as people with common sense while using their abilities to the optimal level. This book will unravel the mystery of the mind and lead you to the path to enlightenment.

Personal Growth Titles

Invincible Thinking

An Essential Guide for a Lifetime of Growth, success, and Triumph

Hardcover • 208 pages • $16.95
ISBN: 978-1-942125-25-9

In this book, Ryuho Okawa lays out the principles of invincible thinking that will allow us to achieve long-lasting triumph. This powerful and unique philosophy is not only about becoming successful or achieving our goal in life, but also about building the foundation of life that becomes the basis of our life-long, lasting success and happiness.

The Laws of Success

A Spiritual Guide to Turning Your Hopes Into Reality

Paperback • 208 pages • $15.95
ISBN: 978-1-942125-15-0

The Laws of Success offers eight spiritual principles that, when put to practice in our day-to-day life, will help us attain lasting success. The timeless wisdom and practical steps that Okawa offers will guide us through any difficulties and problems we may face in life, and serve as guiding principles for living a positive, constructive, and meaningful life.

The Road to Cultivate Yourself

Follow Your Silent Voice Within to Gain True Wisdom

Paperback • 200 pages • $17.95
ISBN: 978-1-958655-05-4 (Jun. 22, 2023)

In the age of uncertainty, how should we live our lives? This book offers unchanging Truth in the ever-changing world, such as the secrets to become more aware of the spiritual self and how to increase intellectual productivity amidst the rapid changes of the modern age. It is packed with Okawa's crystallized wisdom of life.

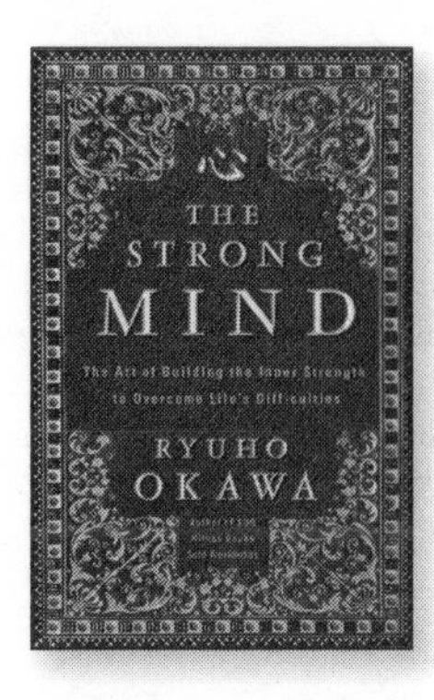

The Strong Mind

The Art of Building the Inner Strength to Overcome Life's Difficulties

Paperback • 192 pages • $15.95
ISBN: 978-1-942125-36-5 (May 25, 2018)

The Strong Mind is what we need to rise time and again and to move forward no matter what difficulties we face in life. This book will inspire and empower you to take courage, cultivate yourself, and achieve resilience and hardiness so that you can break through your limits and keep winning in the battle of your life.

An Unshakable Mind

How to Overcome Life's Difficulties

Paperback • 180 pages • $17.95
ISBN:978-1-942125-91-4 (Nov. 30, 2023)

This book will guide you to build the genuine self-confidence necessary to shape a resilient character and withstand life's turbulence. Author Ryuho Okawa breaks down the cause of life's difficulties and provides solutions to overcome them from the spiritual viewpoint of life based on the laws of the mind.

Worry-Free Living

Let Go of Stress and Live in Peace and Happiness

Hardcover • 192 pages • $16.95
ISBN: 978-1-942125-51-8 (May 15, 2019)

The wisdom Ryuho Okawa shares in this book about facing problems in human relationships, financial hardships, and other life stresses will help you change how you look at and approach life's worries and problems for the better. Let this book be your guide to finding precious meaning in all your life's problems, and to gaining inner growth and happiness.

Words of Wisdom Series

Words for Life

Paperback • 136 pages • $15.95
ISBN: 979-8-88727-089-7 (Mar. 16, 2023)

Ryuho Okawa has written over 3,200 books on various topics. To help readers find the teachings that are beneficial for them out of the extensive teachings, the author has written 100 phrases and put them together. Inside you will find words of wisdom that will help you improve your mindset and lead you to live a meaningful and happy life.

Words for Building Character

Paperback • 140 pages • $15.95
ISBN: 979-8-88737-091-0 (Jun. 21, 2023)

When your life comes to an end, what you can bring with you to the other world is your enlightenment, in other words, the character that you build in this lifetime. If you can read, relish, and truly understand the meaning of these religious phrases, you will be able to attain happiness in this world and the next.

Words to Read in Times of Illness

Hardcover • 136 pages • $17.95
ISBN: 978-1-958655-07-8 (Sep. 15, 2023)

Ryuho Okawa has written 100 Healing Messages to comfort the souls of those going through any illness. When we are ill, it is an ideal time for us to contemplate recent and past events, as well as our relationship with the people around us. It is a chance for us to take inventory of our emotions and thoughts.

Words for Work

Paperback • 140 pages • $15.95
ISBN: 979-8-88737-090-3 (Jul. 20, 2023)

Through his personal experiences at work, Okawa has created these phrases regarding philosophies and practical wisdom about work. This book will be of great use to you throughout your career. Every day you can contemplate and gain tips on how to better your work as well as deepen your insight into company management.

MUSIC BY RYUHO OKAWA

El Cantare Ryuho Okawa Original Songs

A song celebrating Lord God / With Savior

Words & Music by Ryuho Okawa

1. A song celebrating Lord God–Renewal ver.
2. With Savior–Renewal ver.
3. A song celebrating Lord God–Renewal ver. (Instrumental)
4. With Savior–Renewal ver. (Instrumental)
5. With Savior–Renewal ver. (Instrumental with chorus)

To purchase the CD, contact the nearest Happy Science locations.
See p.194 for contact information.

WHO IS EL CANTARE?

El Cantare means "the Light of the Earth." He is the Supreme God of the Earth who has been guiding humankind since the beginning of Genesis, and He is the Creator of the universe. He is whom Jesus called Father and Muhammad called Allah, and is Ame-no-Mioya-Gami, Japanese Father God. Different parts of El Cantare's core consciousness have descended to Earth in the past, once as Alpha and another as Elohim. His branch spirits, such as Shakyamuni Buddha and Hermes, have descended to Earth many times and helped to flourish many civilizations. To unite various religions and to integrate various fields of study in order to build a new civilization on Earth, a part of the core consciousness has descended to Earth as Master Ryuho Okawa.

Alpha is a part of the core consciousness of El Cantare who descended to Earth around 330 million years ago. Alpha preached Earth's Truths to harmonize and unify Earth-born humans and space people who came from other planets.

Elohim is a part of the core consciousness of El Cantare who descended to Earth around 150 million years ago. He gave wisdom, mainly on the differences between light and darkness, good and evil.

Ame-no-Mioya-Gami (Japanese Father God) is the Creator God and the Father God who appears in the ancient literature, *Hotsuma Tsutae*. It is believed that He descended on the foothills of Mt. Fuji about 30,000 years ago and built the Fuji dynasty, which is the root of the Japanese civilization. With justice as the central pillar, Ame-no-Mioya-Gami's teachings spread to ancient civilizations of other countries in the world.

Shakyamuni Buddha was born as a prince into the Shakya clan in India around 2,600 years ago. When he was 29 years old, he renounced the world and sought enlightenment. He later attained Great Enlightenment and founded Buddhism.

Hermes is one of the 12 Olympian gods in Greek mythology, but the spiritual Truth is that he taught the teachings of love and progress around 4,300 years ago which became the origin of the current Western civilization. He is a hero who truly existed.

Ophealis was born in Greece around 6,500 years ago and was the leader who took an expedition to as far as Egypt. He is the God of miracles, prosperity, and arts, and is known as Osiris in Egyptian mythology.

Rient Arl Croud was born as a king of the ancient Incan Empire around 7,000 years ago and taught about the mysteries of the mind. In the heavenly world, he is responsible for the interactions that take place between various planets.

Thoth was an almighty leader who built the golden age of the Atlantic civilization around 12,000 years ago. In Egyptian mythology, he is known as God Thoth.

Ra Mu was a leader who built the golden age of the civilization of Mu around 17,000 years ago. As a religious leader and a politician, he ruled by uniting religion and politics.

ABOUT HAPPY SCIENCE

Happy Science is a religious group founded on the faith in El Cantare who is the God of the Earth, and the Creator of the universe. The essence of human beings is the soul that was created by God, and we all are children of God. God is our true parent, so in our souls we have a fundamental desire to "believe in God, love God, and get closer to God." And, we can get closer to God by living with God's Will as our own. In Happy Science, we call this the "Exploration of Right Mind." More specifically, it means to practice the Fourfold Path, which consists of "Love, Wisdom, Self-Reflection, and Progress."

Love: Love means "love that gives," or mercy. God hopes for the happiness of all people. Therefore, living with God's Will as our own means to start by practicing "love that gives."

Wisdom: God's love is boundless. It is important to learn various Truths in order to understand the heart of God.

Self-Reflection: Once you learn the heart of God and the difference between His mind and yours, you should strive to bring your own mind closer to the mind of God—that process is called self-reflection. Self-reflection also includes meditation and prayer.

Progress: Since God hopes for the happiness of all people, you should also make progress in your love, and make an effort to realize utopia in which everyone in your society, country, and eventually all humankind can become happy.

As we practice this Fourfold Path, our souls will advance toward God step by step. That is when we can attain real happiness—our souls' desire to get closer to God comes true.

In Happy Science, we conduct activities to make ourselves happy through belief in Lord El Cantare, and to spread this faith to the world and bring happiness to all. We welcome you to join our activities!

We hold events and activities to help you practice the Fourfold Path at our branches, temples, missionary centers and missionary houses

Love: We hold various volunteering activities. Our members conduct missionary work together as the greatest practice of love.

Wisdom: We offer our comprehensive collection of books of Truth, many of which are available online and at Happy Science locations. In addition, we offer numerous opportunities such as seminars or book clubs to learn the Truth.

Self-Reflection: We offer opportunities to polish your mind through self-reflection, meditation, and prayer. Many members have experienced improvement in their human relationships by changing their own minds.

Progress: We also offer seminars to enhance your power of influence. Because it is also important to do well at work to make society better, we hold seminars to improve your work and management skills.

"The True Words Spoken By Buddha"

"The True Words Spoken By Buddha" is an English sutra given directly from the spirit of Shakyamuni Buddha, who is a part of Master Ryuho Okawa's subconscious. The words in this sutra are not of a mere human being but are the words of God or Buddha sent directly from the ninth dimension, which is the highest realm of the Earth's Spirit World.

"The True Words Spoken By Buddha" is an essential sutra for us to connect and live with God or Buddha's Will as our own.

MEMBERSHIPS

MEMBERSHIP

If you would like to know more about Happy Science, please consider becoming a member. Those who pledge to believe in Lord El Cantare and wish to learn more can join us.

When you become a member, you will receive the following sutras: "The True Words Spoken By Buddha," "Prayer to the Lord" and "Prayer to Guardian and Guiding Spirits."

DEVOTEE MEMBER

If you would like to learn the teachings of Happy Science and walk the path of faith, become a Devotee member who pledges devotion to the Three Treasures, which are Buddha, Dharma, and Sangha. Buddha refers to Lord El Cantare, Master Ryuho Okawa. Dharma refers to Master Ryuho Okawa's teachings. Sangha refers to Happy Science. Devoting to the Three Treasures will let your Buddha nature shine, and you will enter the path to attain true freedom of the mind.

Becoming a devotee means you become Buddha's disciple. You will discipline your mind and act to bring happiness to society.

EMAIL OR **PHONE CALL**

Please see the contact information page.

ONLINE member.happy-science.org/signup/

CONTACT INFORMATION

Happy Science is a worldwide organization with branches and temples around the globe. For full details, visit happy-science.org. The following are some of our main Happy Science locations:

UNITED STATES AND CANADA

New York
79 Franklin St., New York, NY 10013, USA
Phone: 1-212-343-7972
Fax: 1-212-343-7973
Email: ny@happy-science.org
Website: happyscience-usa.org

New Jersey
66 Hudson St., #2R, Hoboken, NJ 07030, USA
Phone: 1-201-313-0127
Email: nj@happy-science.org
Website: happyscience-usa.org

Chicago
2300 Barrington Rd., Suite #400, Hoffman Estates, IL 60169, USA
Phone: 1-630-937-3077
Email: chicago@happy-science.org
Website: happyscience-usa.org

Florida
5208 8th St., Zephyrhills, FL 33542, USA
Phone: 1-813-715-0000
Fax: 1-813-715-0010
Email: florida@happy-science.org
Website: happyscience-usa.org

Atlanta
1874 Piedmont Ave., NE Suite 360-C
Atlanta, GA 30324, USA
Phone: 1-404-892-7770
Email: atlanta@happy-science.org
Website: happyscience-usa.org

San Francisco
525 Clinton St.
Redwood City, CA 94062, USA
Phone & Fax: 1-650-363-2777
Email: sf@happy-science.org
Website: happyscience-usa.org

Los Angeles
1590 E. Del Mar Blvd., Pasadena, CA 91106, USA
Phone: 1-626-395-7775
Fax: 1-626-395-7776
Email: la@happy-science.org
Website: happyscience-usa.org

Orange County
16541 Gothard St. Suite 104
Huntington Beach, CA 92647
Phone: 1-714-659-1501
Email: oc@happy-science.org
Website: happyscience-usa.org

San Diego
7841 Balboa Ave. Suite #202
San Diego, CA 92111, USA
Phone: 1-626-395-7775
Fax: 1-626-395-7776
E-mail: sandiego@happy-science.org
Website: happyscience-usa.org

Hawaii
Phone: 1-808-591-9772
Fax: 1-808-591-9776
Email: hi@happy-science.org
Website: happyscience-usa.org

Kauai
3343 Kanakolu Street, Suite 5
Lihue, HI 96766, USA
Phone: 1-808-822-7007
Fax: 1-808-822-6007
Email: kauai-hi@happy-science.org
Website: happyscience-usa.org

Toronto
845 The Queensway
Etobicoke, ON M8Z 1N6, Canada
Phone: 1-416-901-3747
Email: toronto@happy-science.org
Website: happy-science.ca

Vancouver
#201-2607 East 49th Avenue,
Vancouver, BC, V5S 1J9, Canada
Phone: 1-604-437-7735
Fax: 1-604-437-7764
Email: vancouver@happy-science.org
Website: happy-science.ca

INTERNATIONAL

Tokyo
1-6-7 Togoshi, Shinagawa,
Tokyo, 142-0041, Japan
Phone: 81-3-6384-5770
Fax: 81-3-6384-5776
Email: tokyo@happy-science.org
Website: happy-science.org

London
3 Margaret St.
London, W1W 8RE United Kingdom
Phone: 44-20-7323-9255
Fax: 44-20-7323-9344
Email: eu@happy-science.org
Website: www.happyscience-uk.org

Sydney
516 Pacific Highway, Lane Cove North,
2066 NSW, Australia
Phone: 61-2-9411-2877
Fax: 61-2-9411-2822
Email: sydney@happy-science.org

Sao Paulo
Rua. Domingos de Morais 1154,
Vila Mariana, Sao Paulo SP
CEP 04010-100, Brazil
Phone: 55-11-5088-3800
Email: sp@happy-science.org
Website: happyscience.com.br

Jundiai
Rua Congo, 447, Jd. Bonfiglioli
Jundiai-CEP, 13207-340, Brazil
Phone: 55-11-4587-5952
Email: jundiai@happy-science.org

Seoul
74, Sadang-ro 27-gil,
Dongjak-gu, Seoul, Korea
Phone: 82-2-3478-8777
Fax: 82-2-3478-9777
Email: korea@happy-science.org

Taipei
No. 89, Lane 155, Dunhua N. Road,
Songshan District, Taipei City 105, Taiwan
Phone: 886-2-2719-9377
Fax: 886-2-2719-5570
Email: taiwan@happy-science.org

Taichung
No. 146, Minzu Rd., Central Dist.,
Taichung City 400001, Taiwan
Phone: 886-4-22233777
Email: taichung@happy-science.org

Kuala Lumpur
No 22A, Block 2, Jalil Link Jalan Jalil Jaya
2, Bukit Jalil 57000,
Kuala Lumpur, Malaysia
Phone: 60-3-8998-7877
Fax: 60-3-8998-7977
Email: malaysia@happy-science.org
Website: happyscience.org.my

Kathmandu
Kathmandu Metropolitan City,
Ward No. 15, Ring Road, Kimdol,
Sitapaila Kathmandu, Nepal
Phone: 977-1-537-2931
Email: nepal@happy-science.org

Kampala
Plot 877 Rubaga Road, Kampala
P.O. Box 34130 Kampala, Uganda
Email: uganda@happy-science.org

ABOUT HAPPINESS REALIZATION PARTY

The Happiness Realization Party (HRP) was founded in May 2009 by Master Ryuho Okawa as part of the Happy Science Group. HRP strives to improve Japanese society, based on three basic political principles of "freedom, democracy, and faith," and let Japan promote individual and public happiness from Asia to the world as a leader nation.

1) Diplomacy and Security: Protecting Freedom, Democracy, and Faith of Japan and the World from China's Totalitarianism

Japan's current defense system is insufficient against China's expanding hegemony and the threat of North Korea's nuclear missiles. Japan, as the leader of Asia, must strengthen its defense power and promote strategic diplomacy together with the nations that share the values of freedom, democracy, and faith. Further, HRP aims to realize world peace under the leadership of Japan, a nation with the spirit of religious tolerance.

2) Economy: Early economic recovery through utilizing the "wisdom of the private sector"

The economy has been damaged severely since the outbreak of the novel coronavirus originated in China. Many companies have been forced into bankruptcy or out of business. What is needed for economic recovery now is not subsidies and regulations by the government, but policies that can utilize the "wisdom of the private sector."

For more information, visit en.hr-party.jp

HAPPY SCIENCE ACADEMY JUNIOR AND SENIOR HIGH SCHOOL

Happy Science Academy Junior and Senior High School is a boarding school founded with the goal of educating the future leaders of the world who can have a big vision, persevere, and take on new challenges.

Currently, there are two campuses in Japan; the Nasu Main Campus in Tochigi Prefecture, founded in 2010, and the Kansai Campus in Shiga Prefecture, founded in 2013.

HAPPY SCIENCE UNIVERSITY

THE FOUNDING SPIRIT AND THE GOAL OF EDUCATION

Based on the founding philosophy of the university, "Exploration of happiness and the creation of a new civilization," education, research and studies will be provided to help students acquire a deep understanding grounded in religious belief and advanced expertise with the objectives of producing "great talents of virtue" who can contribute in a broad-ranging way to serve Japan and the international society.

FACULTIES

Faculty of human happiness

Students in this faculty will pursue liberal arts from various perspectives with a multidisciplinary approach, explore and envision an ideal state of human beings and society.

Faculty of successful management

This faculty aims to realize successful management that helps organizations to create value and wealth for society and to contribute to the happiness and development of management and employees as well as society as a whole.

Faculty of future creation

Students in this faculty study subjects such as political science, journalism, performing arts and artistic expression, and explore and present new political and cultural models based on truth, goodness and beauty.

Faculty of future industry

This faculty aims to nurture engineers who can resolve various issues facing modern civilization from a technological standpoint and contribute to the creation of new industries of the future.

ABOUT IRH PRESS USA INC.

Founded in 2013, New York-based IRH Press USA, Inc. is the North American affiliate of IRH Press Co., Ltd., Japan. The Press exclusively publishes comprehensive titles on Spiritual Truth, religious enrichment, Buddhism, personal growth, and contemporary commentary by Ryuho Okawa, the author of more than 3,200 unique publications, with hundreds of millions of copies sold worldwide. For more information, visit Okawabooks.com.

Follow us on:

Facebook: Okawa Books
Youtube: Okawa Books
Pinterest: Okawa Books
Instagram: OkawaBooks
Twitter: Okawa Books
Goodreads: Ryuho Okawa

NEWSLETTER

To receive book-related news, promotions and events, please subscribe to our newsletter below.

okawabooks.com/pages/subscribe

AUDIO / VISUAL MEDIA

OKAWA BOOK CLUB

YOUTUBE

PODCAST

Introduction of Ryuho Okawa's titles; topics ranging from self-help, current affairs, spirituality, religion, and the universe.